Betty Crocker
BEST-LOVED COOKY
TREASURES

Illustrations by Eric Mulvany

This edition published by arrangement with Wiley Inc.

Printed in the United States of America.

Material in this book has previously been published by Wiley Inc. as *Betty Crocker's Cooky Book* (1963).

Contact the Library of Congress for complete Cataloging-in-Publication Data.

For consistent baking results, the Betty Crocker Kitchens recommend Gold Medal Flour.

For more great ideas, visit www.bettycrocker.com

Art Director: Edward P. Diehl

Dear Friend,

There is no aroma quite so inviting as that of cookies baking, whether ginger or chocolate or caramel. And there is no snack quite so satisfying as two or three fresh-from-the-oven cookies with a cool glass of milk. Nor is there a gift quite so welcome as a lovingly wrapped package from home, brimming with cookies.

In this book you'll find cookies in variety, cherished recipes from the past and recipes using the newest convenience products, hearty-fruit-filled cookies and dainty decorated ones. First come the basic how-to's of cooky-making called the Cooky Primer. The Family Favorites chapter is chock full of cookies for lunchtime, snacktime, anytime—such good eating that we call them disappearing cookies. Following are Company-Best Cookies for teatime, some of them from far-off lands.

Remembering the motto "happy the home with the full cooky jar," we hope you'll turn to this book often.

Cordially,

Betty Crocker®

Table of Contents

Cooky Primer

This is a basic guide to baking perfect cookies. Follow these "hints and helps" to achieve professional, party-proud results with a variety of America's most-made cookies. Even experienced homemakers may welcome this little refresher course leading to the ever-full cooky jar which makes your kitchen the most popular room in your home.

Necessary Utensils

Measuring spoons

Graduated measuring cups

Liquid measuring cups

Mixing bowls

Wooden spoon

Rotary egg beater or
  electric mixer

Baking sheets and pans. (Use
  baking sheets or pans at least
  2″ narrower and shorter
  than oven so heat will
  circulate around them. Shiny,
  bright sheets and pans are
  best for delicate browning.)

Spatula...for removing cookies
  from baking sheet to
  cooling rack

Timer

Cooling racks...to prevent
  soggy cookies

How to Measure Flour by Dipping

*Use this easy time-saving method or the traditional
sifting method, whichever you prefer.*

1 Dip graduated measuring cups
into flour sack or canister.

2 Level off with spatula or straight-
edged knife. Do not tap cup or pack
more flour into cup before leveling
off.

3 Pour flour into mixing bowl with
other ingredients. Or stir flour and
other dry ingredients together.

Baking Hints

1 Use unsalted fat for greasing baking sheets and pans.
Check recipe, as some rich cookies need not be baked
on greased sheets.

2 Try to make all cookies in a batch the same size to
insure uniform baking.

3 Bake a test cooky to see if consistency of dough is
right. If cooky spreads more than desired, add 1 to 2
more tbsp. flour. If cooky seems dry or crumbly, add 1
to 2 tbsp. cream to dough.

4 If baking one sheet of cookies at a time, bake in
center of oven. If baking two sheets, place oven racks
so oven is divided in thirds.

5 Look at cookies when minimum baking time is up.
Try not to overbake. Remove from baking sheet to
cooling rack with spatula immediately because cookies
continue to bake until removed from baking sheet.

6 If possible, have a second cool baking sheet ready
as cooky dough spreads on a hot baking sheet.

How to Store Cookies

Store crisp, thin cookies in container with loose cover.
Store soft cookies in container with a tight-fitting cover.

How to Freeze Cookies

Baked cookies and cooky dough may be stored frozen
9 to 12 months. Pack baked cookies in a rigid box, lin-
ing the box and separating each layer of cookies with
transparent plastic wrap. The clinging quality of the
plastic keeps air from reaching and drying out the
cookies. Shape refrigerator cooky dough in roll; wrap
in foil or transparent plastic wrap. Place drop or
rolled cooky dough in frozen food container or wrap in
foil or transparent plastic wrap.

Can Self-Rising Flour Be Used for Cookies?

Yes, Gold Medal Self-Rising Flour can be used for
baking cookies. Though usually used for quick breads,
it can also be used for other bakings. However, since
leavening and salt are already in the flour, special ad-
justments need to be made. Directions for these adjust-
ments appear in a note below each recipe for a cooky
made with flour in this book.

What Causes Dry Cooky Dough?

There are a number of possible causes. Study the list below, then reread your recipe and you should be able to find the cause.

1 Overmeasurement of flour or dryness of flour. The properties which make flour a "structure builder" in baking also make it absorb and release moisture from the air very readily. Flour stored in a warm, dry kitchen absorbs more moisture (water, milk, or egg) than flour stored in a humid kitchen; thus, it makes a drier dough.

2 Undermeasurement of shortening or use of chilled shortening. If shortening (butter, margarine, or soft shortening) is firm, dough will be less pliable than if shortening is at room temperature.

3 Undermeasurement of liquid or use of small eggs. In some cooky recipes, eggs are the only source of moisture.

How Can Dry Cooky Dough Be Corrected?

Work 1 or 2 tbsp. soft butter or cream into dough with your hands.

How Can Dry Cooky Dough Be Prevented?

1 Measure all ingredients carefully and accurately, using standard measuring cups and spoons.

2 Have shortening at room temperature. However, shortening should not be melted.

What Causes Soft Cooky Dough?

A variety of factors may cause soft doughs which are too soft to roll or spread when baked. They are:

1 Undermeasurement of flour or use of flour that has been stored when humidity was high.

2 Overmeasurement of shortening, butter, or margarine or use of extremely soft or melted shortening.

3 Overmeasurement of liquid or use of extremely large eggs.

4 Dough mixed in a very warm room.

How Can Soft Cooky Dough Be Corrected?

Chill dough until firm enough to handle; then work with it in small portions, leaving rest of dough in refrigerator until needed. If dough is still soft after chilling, work in more flour, one tablespoon at a time; then bake a test cooky.

How Can Soft Cooky Dough Be Prevented?

1 Measure each ingredient accurately and follow mixing directions exactly.

2 Use soft butter, shortening, or margarine; do not use melted shortening.

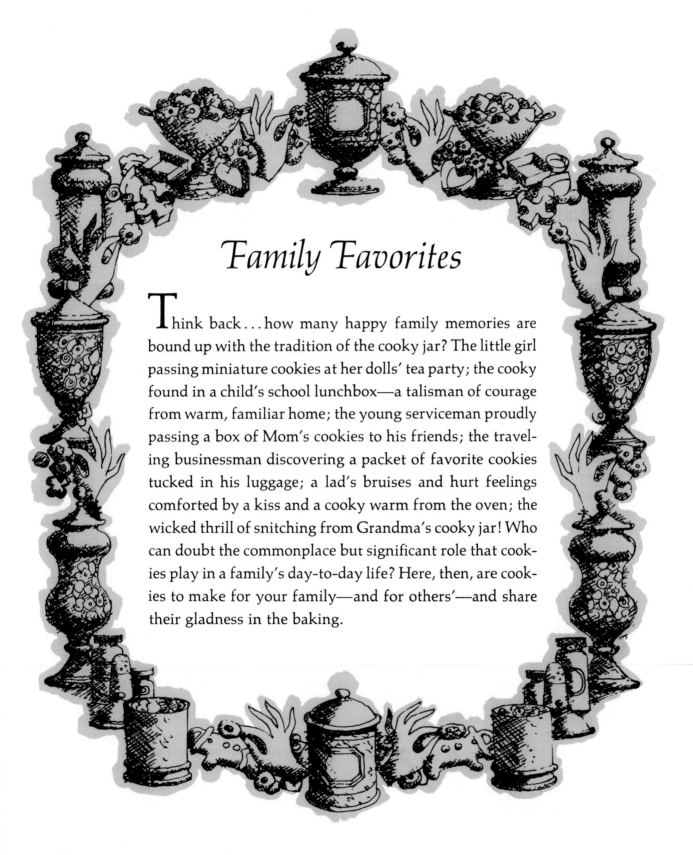

Family Favorites

Think back...how many happy family memories are bound up with the tradition of the cooky jar? The little girl passing miniature cookies at her dolls' tea party; the cooky found in a child's school lunchbox—a talisman of courage from warm, familiar home; the young serviceman proudly passing a box of Mom's cookies to his friends; the traveling businessman discovering a packet of favorite cookies tucked in his luggage; a lad's bruises and hurt feelings comforted by a kiss and a cooky warm from the oven; the wicked thrill of snitching from Grandma's cooky jar! Who can doubt the commonplace but significant role that cookies play in a family's day-to-day life? Here, then, are cookies to make for your family—and for others'—and share their gladness in the baking.

Children love cookies. And mothers—not to mention grandmothers, friends, and neighbors—love to bake cookies for children. Here are Storybook Cookies to bake and enjoy while retelling childhood's favorite tales. Nutritious and delicious cookies for growing youngsters are included, of course, though every chapter of this book has cookies children love. You'll also find complete directions for a Cooky House constructed of packaged cookies—a perfect party centerpiece.

MONKEY-FACED COOKIES

Children can hardly wait until these cookies are out of the oven to see the comical expressions that the raisin faces have taken on in baking.

½ cup shortening
1 cup brown sugar
  (packed)
½ cup molasses
½ cup milk
1 tsp. vinegar

2½ cups Gold Medal
  Flour
1 tsp. soda
½ tsp. salt
½ tsp. ginger
½ tsp. cinnamon
raisins

Heat oven to 375° (quick mod.). Mix shortening, sugar, and molasses thoroughly. Mix milk and vinegar; stir in. Measure flour by dipping method (p. 5) or by sifting. Stir dry ingredients together; blend into sugar mixture. Drop rounded teaspoonfuls of dough 2½" apart on ungreased baking sheet. Place 3 raisins on each for eyes and mouth. Bake 10 to 12 min., or until set. Allow to remain on baking sheet 1 min. before removing. The faces take on droll expressions in baking. *Makes about 4 doz. 2½" cookies.*

Note: *If you use Gold Medal Self-Rising Flour, omit salt and reduce soda to ¼ tsp.*

MALTED MILK ROUNDS

4 cups Gold Medal
  Flour
¾ cup malted milk
  powder (plain)
2 tsp. baking powder
½ tsp. soda
½ tsp. salt
1 cup butter or
  margarine

2 cups brown sugar
  (packed)
2 eggs
⅓ cup commercial
  sour cream
2 tsp. vanilla
Malt Frosting (below)

Measure flour by dipping method (p. 5) or by sifting. Blend first five ingredients thoroughly. Cream butter; gradually add sugar. Blend in eggs; beat well. Add half the blended dry ingredients; mix thoroughly. Add sour cream and vanilla; stir in remaining dry ingredients. Chill at least 4 hr.

Heat oven to 375° (quick mod.). Divide dough and roll ¼" thick on well-floured pastry cloth. Cut with 2½" cutter. Bake 12 to 15 min. on ungreased baking sheet. Cool about 2 min. Remove to racks. Cool; frost tops with Frosting. *Makes about 5 doz. cookies.*

Note: *If you use Gold Medal Self-Rising Flour, omit soda and salt.*

Malt Frosting

½ cup brown sugar
  (packed)
¼ cup butter or
  margarine
¼ cup milk or cream

⅓ cup malted milk
  powder (plain)
½ tsp. vanilla
3 cups sifted
  confectioners'
  sugar

Cook brown sugar, butter, and milk in saucepan until sugar is melted. Remove from heat; stir in malted milk powder and vanilla. Blend in confectioners' sugar gradually until of right consistency.

ALICE'S OATMEAL ROUNDS

Crunchy, sugar-topped cookies. The recipe came from Alice Totushek, whose five lively youngsters request them regularly.

1 cup sugar	½ cup raisins
1 cup shortening (half butter or margarine)	1¾ cups Gold Medal Flour
2 eggs	1 tsp. soda
1 tsp. vanilla	½ tsp. salt
1 cup rolled oats	½ tsp. cinnamon

Mix sugar, shortening, eggs, and vanilla thoroughly. Measure flour by dipping method (p. 5) or by sifting. Blend rest of ingredients into shortening mixture. Refrigerate 4 to 5 hr. or overnight.

Heat oven to 375° (quick mod.). Roll dough in 1″ balls. Place on ungreased baking sheet. Flatten with greased bottom of glass dipped in sugar. Bake 10 min. *Makes 4½ doz. cookies.*

Note: *If you use Gold Medal Self-Rising Flour, omit soda and salt.*

GOLDEN CARROT COOKIES

Mysterious flavor—moist and flavorful. Next time you cook carrots for dinner, add an extra cup for use in these cookies.

1 cup shortening (part butter or margarine)	2 tsp. baking powder
¾ cup sugar	½ tsp. salt
2 eggs	¾ cup shredded coconut
1 cup mashed cooked carrots	Orange Butter Icing (p. 60)
2 cups Gold Medal Flour	

Heat oven to 400° (mod. hot). Mix shortening, sugar, eggs, and carrots. Measure flour by dipping method (p. 5) or by sifting. Blend flour, baking powder, and salt into shortening mixture. Mix in coconut. Drop dough by teaspoonfuls about 2″ apart on lightly greased baking sheet. Bake 8 to 10 min., or until no imprint remains when touched lightly. Frost cooled cookies with Icing. *Makes 4 doz. cookies.*

Note: *If you use Gold Medal Self-Rising Flour, omit baking powder and salt.*

LOLLIPOP COOKIES

Make Mary's Sugar Cookies (p. 18)—except cut 2½ to 3″ circles. Bake 7 to 8 min. in 375° (quick mod.) oven. Cool.

To make lollipop: prepare a triple recipe of Easy Creamy Icing (p. 60); spread on plain baked cooky. Place a flat wooden stick or colored plastic straw across the middle, letting one end extend beyond edge of cooky. Place another cooky on top; press down slightly. Decorate with faces of tinted icing. *Makes about 2 doz. lollipops.*

TRAFFIC LIGHT COOKIES

Make these to help the children learn that it is red for "stop" and green for "go."

Make dough for Ethel's Sugar Cookies (p. 18). Heat oven to 400° (mod. hot). Divide dough in 3 parts. Roll to ¼″ thick on well-floured cloth-covered board. Cut in either 3x2″ rectangles with a knife, or 3″ circles with cooky cutter. Using a thimble, make three indentations in cookies. Place on ungreased baking sheet. Bake 6 to 8 min., or until very lightly browned. When cookies are browned, reinforce indentations with thimble. Place 3 to 4 tbsp. orange marmalade in each of 3 cups. Tint one red, one green; the other is already yellow. Fill indentations with colored marmalade, giving the effect of a traffic light. *Makes 2½ to 3 doz. cookies.*

CHEERIOS MOLASSES PATTIES

If your children like caramel corn, they'll love these crispy confections. See color picture opposite.

4 cups Cheerios	**½ cup water**
1½ cups salted peanuts	**1 tbsp. plus 1 tsp.**
1½ cups brown sugar	**vinegar**
(packed)	**⅛ tsp. cream of tartar**
¾ cup light molasses	**1½ tsp. soda**

Measure Cheerios and peanuts into large greased bowl. Mix sugar, molasses, water, vinegar, and cream of tartar in saucepan. Cook over low heat, stirring occasionally, to hard ball stage (250°). (A hard ball forms when a small amount of syrup is dropped into cold water.) Remove from heat. Blend in soda; mixture becomes fluffy and porous. Pour syrup over Cheerios-peanut mixture. Mix well with greased spoon. Allow to cool slightly to thicken. With greased hands, form mixture in patties. Cool on a greased baking sheet or waxed paper. *Makes about 3 doz. 2" patties.*

WHEATIES CHERRY BLINKS

These rich, Wheaties-coated, cherry-topped cookies are just the thing for parties. See color picture opposite.

⅓ cup shortening	**¼ tsp. salt**
½ cup sugar	**½ cup raisins or**
1 egg	**cut-up dates**
1½ tbsp. milk	**½ cup nuts, chopped**
½ tsp. vanilla	**1½ cups Wheaties,**
1 cup Gold Medal Flour	**crushed**
½ tsp. baking powder	**candied or maraschino**
¼ tsp. soda	**cherries**

Heat oven to 375° (quick mod.). Mix shortening, sugar, and egg. Stir in milk and vanilla. Measure flour by dipping method (p. 5) or by sifting. Blend dry ingredients together; stir in. Mix in raisins and nuts. Drop dough by teaspoonfuls into Wheaties. Roll gently so balls of dough are completely coated. Place about 2" apart on greased baking sheet. Top with a piece of cherry. Bake 10 to 12 min., or until no imprint remains when touched lightly. *Makes about 3 doz. cookies.*

Note: *If you use Gold Medal Self-Rising Flour, omit baking powder, soda, and salt.*

TRIX COOKIES

See color picture opposite.

¾ cup butter or	**1½ cups Gold Medal**
margarine	**Flour**
1½ cups sugar	**½ tsp. soda**
1 egg	**1 tsp. salt**
1 tsp. almond extract	**1 cup rolled oats**
¼ cup water	**4 cups Trix cereal**

Heat oven to 375° (quick mod.). Mix butter, sugar, egg, flavoring, and water well. Measure flour by dipping method (p. 5) or by sifting. Blend flour, soda, salt; add to the sugar mixture. Mix in rolled oats and Trix. Drop by spoonfuls on greased baking sheet. Bake 10 to 12 min. *Makes 5 doz. cookies.*

Note: *If you use Gold Medal Self-Rising Flour, omit soda and salt.*

COCOA PUFF BALLS

See color picture opposite.

1 cup sugar	**1½ sq. unsweetened**
⅓ cup water	**chocolate (1½ oz.)**
⅓ cup light corn syrup	**1 tsp. vanilla**
1 tsp. salt	**8 cups Cocoa Puffs**
¼ cup butter or	**cereal**
margarine	

Mix sugar, water, corn syrup, salt, butter, and chocolate in saucepan. Heat until chocolate is melted. Bring to boil; cook to 250° on candy thermometer or until a few drops form a hard ball when dropped in cold water. Remove from heat. Stir in vanilla. Pour hot syrup over Cocoa Puffs in large buttered bowl. Stir constantly to distribute syrup. Form in balls with buttered hands. If balls pull apart, reshape occasionally until they harden. *Makes 16 large balls.*

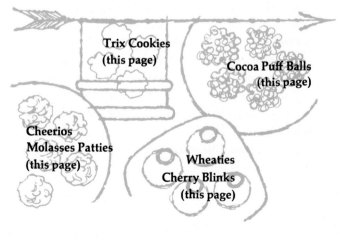

Trix Cookies (this page)

Cocoa Puff Balls (this page)

Cheerios Molasses Patties (this page)

Wheaties Cherry Blinks (this page)

PEANUT THINS

An all-around good family cooky...yet attractive enough to serve to company, too.

¾ cup shortening (part butter or margarine)
1 cup brown sugar (packed)
¼ cup peanut butter
1 egg yolk
1 tsp. vanilla

1¾ cups Gold Medal Flour
Thin Confectioners' Sugar Icing (p. 61)
½ cup chopped salted peanuts

Heat oven to 350° (mod.). Mix shortening, sugar, peanut butter, egg yolk, and vanilla until light and fluffy. Measure flour by dipping method (p. 5) or by sifting. Add flour; mix thoroughly. Knead dough with hands to form a ball. Divide dough into 2 parts. With floured rolling pin, roll each part on a separate ungreased baking sheet into 12x6" strip (be sure edges aren't too thin). Bake 13 to 14 min., or until lightly browned and set. While warm, spread with Icing. Sprinkle with chopped peanuts. Cut in bars, 3x1". *Makes 4 doz. bars.*

Note: *You may use Gold Medal Self-Rising Flour in this recipe.*

QUICK PEANUT THINS

Make Peanut Thins (above)—except do not divide dough. Pat evenly into ungreased jelly roll pan, 15½x 10½x1". Bake 18 min. Finish as above. *Makes 30 bars.*

CRUNCHY NUT COOKIES

1 cup granulated sugar
1 cup brown sugar (packed)
½ cup shortening
2 eggs

1 tsp. vanilla
3 cups Gold Medal Flour
1 tsp. soda
½ tsp. salt
1 cup chopped nuts

Heat oven to 375° (quick mod.). Mix thoroughly sugars, shortening, eggs, and vanilla. Measure flour by dipping method (p. 5) or by sifting. Blend flour, soda, and salt; stir in. Add nuts. Form in 1" balls. (Dough will be dry.) Place on ungreased baking sheet. Flatten with bottom of greased glass dipped in sugar. Bake 8 to 10 min. *Makes about 5 doz. cookies.*

Note: *If you use Gold Medal Self-Rising Flour, omit soda and salt.*

STIR-N-DROP OATMEAL COOKIES

1 cup Gold Medal Flour
1 tsp. baking powder
½ tsp. salt
½ tsp. cinnamon
½ tsp. ginger
1 cup brown sugar (packed)

1 cup rolled oats
¼ cup vegetable oil
2 tbsp. milk
1 egg
¾ cup Spanish peanuts, if desired

Heat oven to 375° (quick mod.). Measure flour by dipping method (p. 5) or by sifting. Stir dry ingredients together; add sugar and rolled oats. Mix in oil, milk, and egg thoroughly. Add peanuts. Drop teaspoonfuls of dough about 2" apart on lightly greased baking sheet. Bake about 10 min. *Makes about 3 doz. cookies.*

Note: *If you use Gold Medal Self-Rising Flour, omit baking powder and salt.*

BRAZILIAN NUT COOKIES

A good, not-too-sweet cooky for young children.

1 cup Gold Medal Flour	1 egg
½ cup sugar	¼ cup milk
2 tsp. baking powder	2 tsp. lemon juice
½ tsp. salt	1 cup chopped Brazil
2 tbsp. shortening	nuts

Heat oven to 375° (quick mod.). Measure flour by dipping method (p. 5) or by sifting. Stir dry ingredients together. Add other ingredients except nuts; mix vigorously until well blended. Stir in nuts. Drop rounded teaspoonfuls of dough about 3″ apart on lightly greased baking sheet. Bake 8 to 12 min., or until lightly browned. *Makes 2½ to 3 doz. cookies.*

Note: *If you use Gold Medal Self-Rising Flour, omit baking powder and salt.*

PEANUT COOKIES

Make Brazilian Nut Cookies (above)—except use chopped salted peanuts in place of Brazil nuts.

OATSIES

A delicious caramel-like oat confection topped with chocolate. Shared with us by Charlotte Johnson of our staff, who makes them often for her college-student son and daughter.

2 cups rolled oats	½ tsp. salt
½ cup brown sugar (packed)	1 tsp. vanilla
½ cup butter or margarine	1 pkg. (6 oz.) semi-sweet chocolate pieces
¼ cup dark corn syrup	¼ cup chopped nuts

Heat oven to 400° (mod. hot). Mix oats and sugar. Melt butter; add syrup, salt, and vanilla. Pour over the oats and sugar; mix well. Pat out in greased square pan, 9x9x1¾″. Bake 8 to 10 min. Do not overbake! It will be bubbly when done. While this cools, melt chocolate. Spread on chocolate; sprinkle with nuts. Cut into bars. *Makes 32 bars.*

WHEATIES NUT DROPS

A simple stir-up-and-drop cooky. Mother may want to do the actual baking, but children can do the rest.

½ cup shortening	1 tsp. baking powder
1 cup brown sugar (packed)	½ tsp. salt
2 eggs	1 cup nuts, coarsely chopped
1 tsp. vanilla	4 cups Wheaties
1¼ cups Gold Medal Flour	

Heat oven to 375° (quick mod.). Mix shortening, sugar, eggs, and vanilla together thoroughly. Measure flour by dipping method (p. 5) or by sifting. Stir flour, baking powder, and salt together. Blend shortening and flour mixtures. Stir in nuts. Carefully fold in Wheaties. Drop by teaspoonfuls about 3″ apart on lightly greased baking sheet. Bake 8 to 10 min. *Makes 4 to 5 doz. cookies.*

Note: *If you use Gold Medal Self-Rising Flour, omit baking powder and salt.*

PECAN CRISPS

Crisp, thin, nutty wafers with attractive glazed surface.

1½ cups Gold Medal Flour	1 egg, separated
1 cup sugar	3 tbsp. milk
¾ tsp. salt	1 tsp. vanilla
½ cup shortening (part butter or margarine)	1 cup pecans, finely chopped

Measure flour by dipping method (p. 5) or by sifting. Blend flour, sugar, and salt in bowl. Mix in shortening, egg yolk, milk, and vanilla thoroughly with fork. Chill dough.

Heat oven to 375° (quick mod.). Form dough in 1″ balls. Place on ungreased baking sheet. Press 1/16″ thick with bottom of greased glass dipped in sugar. Dough must be pressed very thin so cooky is wafer-like; otherwise it will be too chewy. Brush with slightly beaten egg white. Sprinkle with pecans. Bake 8 to 10 min. Do not overbake! *Makes about 5 doz. cookies.*

Note: *If you use Gold Medal Self-Rising Flour, omit salt.*

COOKY HOUSE

USE THESE MATERIALS:

FOR HOUSE

Frame . . . . .1 cardboard box, at least 21x20x13"; cellophane tape or masking tape

Cement for Walls . . .3 recipes of pink Frosting "Cement" (p. 61); 2 recipes of yellow Frosting "Cement" (p. 61);

Bricks for Walls . . . .2 lb. chocolate-covered cream wafer sticks (3x½x½")

Stones for Gable . . .1 pkg. (1 lb.) Dutch apple cookies or vanilla cooky pops (about 1⅜" diameter)

Shingles for Roof . . .3 pkg. (10½ oz. each) lemon thins or brown-edged wafers (about 2" diameter)

Chimney . . . . .1 small pkg. pink party mints, shaved to make one side flat

Chimney Stacks . . .1¾" piece peppermint stick (1" diameter); *and* 1¼" piece peppermint stick (½" diameter)

Windows . . . . .6 scalloped rectangular tea cookies (2¼x 1½"), decorated with icing (mix ¼ cup confectioners' sugar and ¾ tsp. milk) for window panes

Shutters . . . . .12 pink sugar wafers, cut lengthwise to ¾" widths

Doors . . . . .2 long fig newton bars (3⅝x1½"—available at soda fountains)

Door Windows . . . . .8 pink party mints, shaved to make one side flat

Door Handles . . . . . .2 red cinnamon candies

Light Fixtures . . . . . .2 small yellow gumdrops

FOR YARD

Grass . . . . .¾ lb. coconut, soaked in green water (colored by food coloring), then dried

Animals . . . . .chocolate animals or animal crackers coated with melted chocolate

Trees . . . . .ice cream cones frosted with 1 recipe white Frosting "Cement" (p. 61) and trimmed with decorators' sugar

Path . . . . .1 small pkg. yellow party mints

Fence . . . . .piece of cardboard (6x2") and 1 small pkg. assorted party mints

Flowers . . . . .small round gumdrops, ring gumdrops, large square gumdrops, candy mint leaves

Flower Garden . . . . .candy-coated chocolate candies

DIRECTIONS

1. Cut frame for house, roof, chimney, and chimney top from flattened cardboard box (see diagram), using a single-edged razor blade; fold up sides of house and chimney (dotted lines on diagram); tape corners in place. (If cardboard is hard to fold, lightly score outside of fold with razor blade.)

2. Place house frame (without roof) on large piece of cardboard (2 to 3 ft. sq.) which will serve as base for grass.

3. Working rapidly on one wall at a time, spread pink "cement" ¼" thick. For front and back of house, firmly press bricks, door, and stones into "cement" (see picture opposite), supporting wall with one hand from inside. Repeat for side walls, applying bricks; omit top row to permit roof to fit properly. Put vertical corner bricks in place.

4. Attach roof by frosting a 2" border around entire underside edge with yellow "cement"; hold in place on top of walls for several minutes until set. Spread yellow "cement" ¼" thick on one side of roof at a time. Starting with the bottom row, press top edge of shingles on "cement." Each row overlaps ½ of the row beneath (see picture). Since each row of shingles is not directly over the previous row, every other row requires half a cooky at each roof edge.

5. Test chimney for fit; trim if necessary. Frost entire outside of chimney with pink "cement"; place on roof. (Use "cement" at base of chimney to make it fit the roof peak, if necessary.) Press flat side of mints into "cement" on chimney.

6. Using pink "cement," frost underside of chimney top; hold in place on chimney until set; thickly frost topside of chimney top. Press chimney stacks into "cement."

7. Frost underside of decorated windows thinly with leftover "cement"; put in place. Frost long underside edge of shutter; put in place, allowing to stand out slightly.

8. Attach door handles, door windows, and light fixtures with dabs of "cement."

9. For fence, frost one side of the 6x2" cardboard piece with leftover "cement"; place mints in rows on one side, alternating colors. Repeat on other side. Front top of fence. Set in place.

10. Decorate trees; set in place.

11. To make flowers, force small, round gumdrops into gumdrop ring. Slice mint leaves in half horizontally. Put toothpick through leaves and into bottom of small gumdrop; secure other end of toothpick in square gumdrop. Set in place.

12. Arrange flower garden, animals, and path; sprinkle grass around house.

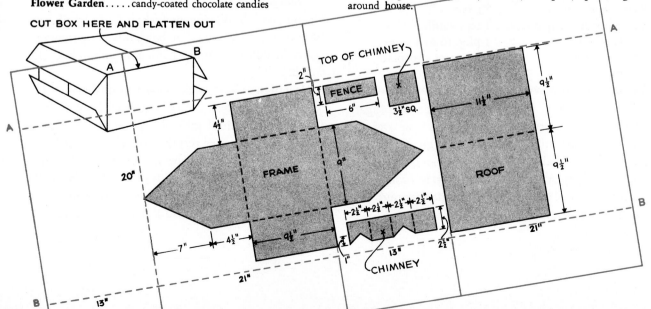

CUT BOX HERE AND FLATTEN OUT

Millions of lunches go off to school and work each day in boxes, pails, and paper bags. And many of these lunches contain cookies—to sweeten the day and provide quick energy for the afternoon ahead.

The ideal lunchbox cooky is appetizing in appearance, flavorful, and satisfying. Always pack cookies in pairs—one for lunch and one to share. Sometimes tuck in a third for an afternoon snack. And, of course, a cooky that's good in a lunchbox is just as delicious eaten for lunch or snacks at home.

NEW NORTHLAND COOKIES

Ruth G. Anderson, former editor of our cook books, brought back this recipe after a scenic cruise via the St. Lawrence River to Labrador.

½ cup shortening (part butter or margarine)	2 cups Gold Medal Flour
	1 tsp. soda
	½ tsp. salt
1 cup brown sugar (packed)	½ tsp. cinnamon
	½ cup cut-up blanched almonds
¼ cup cold water	

Mix shortening and sugar thoroughly. Stir in cold water. Measure flour by dipping method (p. 5) or by sifting. Blend dry ingredients; stir into shortening mixture. Mix in almonds. Mix thoroughly with hands. Press and mold into a long, smooth roll about 2½″ in diameter. Wrap in waxed paper and chill until stiff (several hours or overnight).

Heat oven to 400° (mod. hot). Cut dough in thin slices ⅛ to 1/16″ thick. Place slices a little apart on ungreased baking sheet. Bake 6 to 8 min., until lightly browned. Remove from pan immediately. *Makes about 4 doz. 2½″ cookies.*

Note: *If you use Gold Medal Self-Rising Flour, omit soda and salt.*

SPICED PRUNE COOKIES

Soft, yet chewy . . . made in minutes because prunes are not cooked, just cut or snipped from pits.

½ cup butter or margarine	½ tsp. nutmeg
	½ tsp. cinnamon
1 cup brown sugar (packed)	⅛ tsp. ground cloves
	¼ cup milk
1 egg	1 cup cut-up pitted prunes, uncooked
1¾ cups Gold Medal Flour	½ cup chopped walnuts
½ tsp. soda	
½ tsp. salt	

Mix butter, sugar, and egg. Measure flour by dipping method (p. 5) or by sifting. Blend flour, soda, salt, nutmeg, cinnamon, and cloves. Add to sugar mixture; blend in milk. Add prunes and walnuts, mixing well. Chill 1 hr.

Heat oven to 400° (mod. hot). Drop dough by rounded teaspoonfuls on greased baking sheet. Bake 8 to 10 min. *Makes about 4 doz. cookies.*

Note: *If you use Gold Medal Self-Rising Flour, omit soda and salt.*

CHOCOLATE FRUIT BARS

Delightful for entertaining or as family fare.

1¼ cups Gold Medal Flour
1½ tsp. baking powder
1 tsp. salt
3 eggs
1 cup sugar
½ tsp. almond extract
1 pkg. (6 oz.) semi-sweet chocolate pieces
1 cup chopped dates or raisins
½ cup chopped maraschino cherries, drained
1 cup chopped walnuts

Heat oven to 350° (mod.). Measure flour by dipping method (p. 5) or by sifting. Stir flour, baking powder, and salt together. Beat eggs until light; add sugar gradually, beating well after each addition. Stir in almond flavoring, then dry ingredients. Fold in chocolate pieces, fruits, and nuts. Spread dough evenly in greased oblong pan, 13x9½x2″. Bake 30 to 35 min. If desired, when cool, frost with confectioners' sugar icing. Cut in bars; garnish each bar with a chocolate piece. *Makes 3 doz. bars.*

Note: *If you use Gold Medal Self-Rising Flour, omit baking powder and salt.*

COCONUT APRICOT STRIPS

Fancy and oh-so-rich! Serve tiny bars the same day they are made.

½ cup shortening (half butter or margarine)
½ cup confectioners' sugar
2 egg yolks
1 cup Gold Medal Flour
½ cup thick apricot preserves
½ cup thick pineapple preserves
Coconut Meringue (below)

Heat oven to 350° (mod.). Mix shortening, sugar, and egg yolks thoroughly. Measure flour by dipping method (p. 5) or by sifting. Stir flour into sugar mixture. Press and flatten mixture to cover bottom of ungreased oblong pan, 13x9½x2″. Bake 10 min. Remove from oven and spread with preserves, then with **Meringue**. Return to oven; bake about 20 min., until **Meringue** is golden brown. Cool slightly; cut in small bars, about 2x1″. *Makes about 4 doz. bars.*

Note: *If desired, Gold Medal Self-Rising Flour may be used.*

Coconut Meringue: Beat 2 egg whites until frothy. Gradually add ½ cup sugar; beat until stiff and glossy. Fold in ½ cup flaked coconut.

Chocolate Fruit Bars
(above)

Coconut-Chocolate
Meringue Bites
(p. 52)

Coconut Apricot
Strips (above)

How to Make Perfect Rolled Cookies

Mix dough as directed. Using part of dough and keeping rest chilled, lightly roll dough to desired thickness; the thinner you roll, the crisper the cookies. Rub flour into rolling pin cover and cloth to prevent sticking.

To cut: dip cooky cutter in flour, shake off excess, cut with steady pressure. Cut as many cookies from each rolling as possible. Cut diamonds or squares with knife. Carefully lift cut-out cookies to baking sheet with spatula. Bake.

Perfect rolled cookies have:
- *uniform shape of cutter*
- *lightly browned surface*
- *crisp texture or soft texture, depending on thickness*
- *rich, delicate flavor*

ETHEL'S SUGAR COOKIES

A time-tested family favorite...made with granulated sugar.

¾ cup shortening (part butter or margarine)	2½ cups Gold Medal Flour
1 cup sugar	1 tsp. baking powder
2 eggs	1 tsp. salt
½ tsp. lemon flavoring or 1 tsp. vanilla	

Mix shortening, sugar, eggs, and flavoring thoroughly. Measure flour by dipping method (p. 5) or by sifting. Stir flour, baking powder, and salt together; blend in. Chill at least 1 hr.

Heat oven to 400° (mod. hot). Roll dough ⅛" thick on lightly floured board. Cut with 3" cooky cutter. Place on ungreased baking sheet. Bake 6 to 8 min., or until cookies are a delicate golden color. *Makes about 4 doz. cookies.*

Note: *Do not use Gold Medal Self-Rising Flour in this recipe.*

MARY'S SUGAR COOKIES

From Mary Herman...made with confectioners' sugar.

1½ cups sifted confectioners' sugar	½ tsp. almond flavoring
1 cup butter or margarine	2½ cups Gold Medal Flour
1 egg	1 tsp. soda
1 tsp. vanilla	1 tsp. cream of tartar

Mix sugar and butter. Add egg and flavorings; mix thoroughly. Measure flour by dipping method (p. 5) or by sifting. Stir dry ingredients together and blend in. Refrigerate 2 to 3 hr.

Heat oven to 375° (quick mod.). Divide dough in half and roll 3/16" thick on lightly floured pastry cloth. Cut with cooky cutter; sprinkle with sugar. Place on lightly greased baking sheet. Bake 7 to 8 min., or until delicately golden. *Makes 5 doz. 2 to 2½" cookies.*

Note: *If you use Gold Medal Self-Rising Flour, omit soda and cream of tartar.*

Snowflakes (p. 59)

Buttery Nut Rounds
(p. 51)

CANADIAN HONEY DROPS

These soft brown sugar cookies look just like children's yo-yos when put together in pairs with apricot jam.

1 cup shortening (part butter or margarine)	⅓ cup honey
	1 tsp. vanilla
1 cup brown sugar (packed)	3½ cups Gold Medal Flour
2 eggs	2 tsp. soda
	apricot jam

Mix shortening, sugar, and eggs thoroughly. Stir in honey and vanilla. Measure flour by dipping method (p. 5) or by sifting. Blend together flour and soda; stir in. Chill until firm, several hours or overnight.

Heat oven to 350° (mod.). Roll dough in 1¼" balls. Place on ungreased baking sheet. Bake 10 to 12 min., or until almost no imprint remains when touched lightly. When slightly cooled, put together in pairs with apricot or other jam. *Makes 3 doz. double 2" cookies.*

Note: *If you use Gold Medal Self-Rising Flour, omit soda.*

SUGAR 'N SPICE COOKIES

Sweetness and spice with a tenderness that's nice.

¾ cup shortening	2 tsp. soda
1 cup granulated sugar	¼ tsp. salt
1 egg	1 tsp. cinnamon
¼ cup molasses	¾ tsp. cloves
2 cups Gold Medal Flour	¾ tsp. ginger
	confectioners' sugar

Heat oven to 375° (quick mod.). Mix shortening, sugar, egg, and molasses thoroughly. Measure flour by dipping method (p. 5) or by sifting. Blend dry ingredients; stir into shortening mixture. Form in 1" balls. Place about 2" apart on greased baking sheet. Bake 10 to 12 min. Roll in confectioners' sugar while still warm. *Makes 4 to 5 doz. 2" cookies.*

Note: *If you use Gold Medal Self-Rising Flour, omit salt and reduce soda to ½ tsp.*

COCONUT-CHERRY COOKIES

Attractive, tender; bits of cherry and coconut give color and texture ... from Ruth Brand.

½ cup butter or margarine	½ tsp. soda
	1½ tsp. salt
½ cup shortening	½ cup chopped candied cherries
1 cup sugar	
3 eggs	¼ cup cut-up citron
½ cup commercial sour cream	1 cup shredded coconut
	1 tsp. grated orange rind
3¼ cups Gold Medal Flour	
	1½ tsp. lemon or almond extract
1 tsp. baking powder	

Heat oven to 400° (mod. hot). Mix butter, shortening, sugar, and eggs thoroughly. Stir in sour cream. Measure flour by dipping method (p. 5) or by sifting. Stir dry ingredients together; blend into shortening mixture. Stir in rest of ingredients. Drop dough by rounded teaspoonfuls about 2" apart on ungreased baking sheet. Bake 10 to 12 min., or until lightly browned. *Makes 7 to 8 doz. 2" cookies.*

Note: *If you use Gold Medal Self-Rising Flour, omit baking powder, soda, and salt.*

PEANUT BUTTER CRUNCHIES

A rich cooky with crisp Wheaties coating.

1 cup butter or margarine	1 tsp. vanilla
	1⅓ cups Gold Medal Flour
⅔ cup chunk-style peanut butter	
	½ tsp. soda
1 cup brown sugar (packed)	¼ tsp. salt
	¾ cup crushed Wheaties
1 egg	

Blend butter and peanut butter. Mix in sugar. Stir in egg and vanilla; beat well. Measure flour by dipping method (p. 5) or by sifting. Blend flour, soda, and salt; mix thoroughly into butter-sugar mixture. Refrigerate dough several hours, or until firm.

Heat oven to 350° (mod.). Shape dough into small balls; roll in crushed Wheaties. Place about 2" apart on greased baking sheet. Bake 12 to 15 min. *Makes about 4 doz. cookies.*

Note: *If you use Gold Medal Self-Rising Flour, omit soda and salt.*

COFFEE FRUIT DROPS

Chopped raw apple lends moistness to these cake-like drop cookies. The family will rave about them. See color picture opposite.

2 cups peeled and finely chopped apple	1 tsp. cinnamon
1 cup strong coffee or 1 tbsp. powdered instant coffee dissolved in 1 cup water	¾ tsp. cloves
	¾ tsp. nutmeg
	1 tsp. vanilla
	2 cups Gold Medal Flour
1 cup sugar	1 tsp. soda
½ cup shortening	¼ tsp. salt
1 cup raisins	1 cup chopped walnuts

Cook apple, coffee, sugar, shortening, raisins, and spices in saucepan gently until apple is tender. Remove from heat and cool.

Heat oven to 375° (quick mod.). Add vanilla to cooked mixture. Measure flour by dipping method (p. 5) or by sifting. Blend flour, soda, and salt; stir in. Mix in nuts. Drop by heaping teaspoonfuls on ungreased baking sheet. Bake about 12 min. *Makes about 6 doz. cookies.*

Note: *If you use Gold Medal Self-Rising Flour, omit soda and salt.*

FIG-NUT SQUARES

Moist, rich, chewy cookies with wonderful keeping qualities. See color picture opposite.

2 eggs	½ tsp. baking powder
½ cup sugar	½ tsp. salt
½ tsp. vanilla	1½ cups finely cut-up dried figs
½ cup Gold Medal Flour	1 cup chopped nuts

Heat oven to 350° (mod.). Beat eggs until foamy. Beat in sugar and vanilla. Measure flour by dipping method (p. 5) or by sifting. Blend dry ingredients; mix into egg mixture. Add figs and nuts; spread in greased square pan, 9x9x1¾". Bake 25 to 30 min. *Makes 25 squares.*

DATE-NUT SQUARES

Make Fig-Nut Squares (above)—except use 2 cups finely cut-up dates in place of figs.

RAISIN CRISSCROSS COOKIES

Delicious lemon-flavored raisin cookies...children love them! See color picture opposite.

½ cup shortening (part butter or margarine)	1¾ cups Gold Medal Flour
¾ cup sugar	¾ tsp. cream of tartar
1 egg	¾ tsp. soda
½ tsp. lemon extract	¼ tsp. salt
	1 cup raisins

Heat oven to 400° (mod. hot). Mix thoroughly shortening, sugar, egg, and extract. Measure flour by dipping method (p. 5) or by sifting. Blend flour, cream of tartar, soda, and salt. Stir into shortening mixture. Mix in raisins. Roll in 1" balls. Place about 3" apart on ungreased baking sheet. Flatten with fork dipped in flour, making a crisscross pattern. Bake 8 to 10 min. *Makes about 3 doz. cookies.*

Note: *If you use Gold Medal Self-Rising Flour, omit cream of tartar, soda, and salt.*

CHOCOLATE CRISSCROSS COOKIES

Make Raisin Crisscross Cookies (above)—except substitute ½ cup semi-sweet chocolate pieces for raisins.

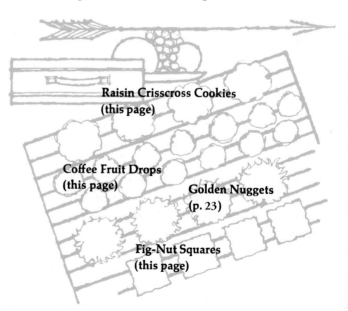

Raisin Crisscross Cookies (this page)

Coffee Fruit Drops (this page)

Golden Nuggets (p. 23)

Fig-Nut Squares (this page)

Cookies are such a thoughtful, personal gift to send to friends away from home, students, or men in the armed services. Here are some helpful hints to insure your cookies' fresh arrival in good condition. So bake some soon to send, with warmest wishes, to someone who is far away...but close to your heart.

What Cookies Travel Best?

Bar cookies, drop cookies, and fruit cookies travel well. Avoid fragile rolled cookies which may crumble before they reach their destination.

What Wrapping Materials Will Be Needed?

Use a sturdy packing box—heavier than ordinary pasteboard. Line with waxed paper. Have plenty of filler: crushed or shredded newspaper, wrapping paper, tissue paper.

Wrap Cookies Carefully.

Wrap each cooky separately in waxed paper or transparent plastic wrap. Or place cookies bottom-to-bottom in pairs and wrap each pair.

Pack Cookies in Layers.

Place a layer of filler in bottom of packing box and cover it with waxed paper. Lay wrapped cookies closely together on waxed paper. Alternate layers of cookies and filling with enough filler over the last layer of cookies to act as padding at the top. The box should be so full that you have to press down the lid to get it on. Remember to enclose a card saying who sent the box of cookies.

Wrap the Box and Address Plainly.

Wrap the box tightly with heavy paper and cord. Address plainly with permanent ink, covering the address with transparent tape or colorless nail polish. Mark the box PERISHABLE AND FRAGILE. Be sure to use the correct amount of postage.

GOLDEN CHEERIOS BARS

Creamy caramel bars with puffed oat cereal, coconut, and peanuts.

4 cups Cheerios	1 cup sugar
1 cup salted peanuts	½ cup corn syrup
1 cup coconut,	1 cup cream (20%
if desired	butterfat)

Mix Cheerios, peanuts, and coconut in large greased bowl. Mix sugar, corn syrup, and cream in saucepan. Cook syrup mixture over low heat, stirring occasionally, to soft ball stage (236°). (Mixture forms a soft ball when a small amount is dropped into cold water.) Remove from heat. Pour syrup mixture over Cheerios mixture. Mix well. Turn out into buttered square pan, 8x8x2″ or 9x9x1¾″. With hand protected by a piece of waxed paper, pat out mixture evenly in pan. Cool. Cut in bars. *Makes thirty-two 2x1″ bars.*

CHOCOLATE CHIP BARS

⅓ cup shortening	¼ tsp. salt
1¼ cups brown sugar	½ cup semi-sweet
(packed)	chocolate pieces
2 eggs	(½ of 6-oz. pkg.)
1¼ cups Gold Medal	½ cup coarsely
Flour	broken nuts
1¼ tsp. baking powder	

Heat oven to 350° (mod.). Mix shortening, sugar, and eggs thoroughly. Measure flour by dipping method (p. 5) or by sifting. Stir dry ingredients together and blend into shortening mixture. Stir in chocolate pieces and nuts. Spread in greased square pan, 9x9x1¾″. Bake 30 to 35 min. When almost cool, cut in bars. *Makes 16 bars.*

Note: *If you use Gold Medal Self-Rising Flour, omit baking powder and salt.*

FROSTY FRUIT SQUARES

Moist, luscious, easy-to-make. Perfect for holiday gift boxes. Candied cherries, candied pineapple, or dates may be used in place of candied fruit.

⅔ cup shortening (part butter)	½ tsp. salt
1 cup sugar	½ tsp. cinnamon
1 egg	½ tsp. nutmeg
1 tbsp. grated orange rind, if desired	1 cup raisins
¼ cup orange or pineapple juice	1 cup mixed candied fruit
2½ cups Gold Medal Flour	½ cup chopped nuts, if desired
1 tsp. soda	Quick Cream Icing (p. 61)

Heat oven to 400° (mod. hot). Mix shortening, sugar, and egg until fluffy. Stir in rind and juice. Measure flour by dipping method (p. 5) or by sifting. Blend dry ingredients and stir into sugar mixture. Mix in fruit and nuts; pat dough evenly into greased jelly roll pan, 15½x10½x1", or into two square pans, one 8x8x2" and one 9x9x1¾". Bake 15 to 18 min., or until top springs back when touched lightly. Cool slightly; spread on Icing. If desired, decorate with bits of candied fruit. Cut in squares. *Makes 3 doz. 2" squares.*

Note: *If you use Gold Medal Self-Rising Flour, omit soda and salt.*

GOLDEN NUGGETS

Full of apricot nuggets. See color picture, p.21.

1 cup dried apricots, coarsely cut up	1 tsp. vanilla
½ cup water	½ tsp. almond flavoring
1 cup shortening (part butter or margarine)	1¾ cups Gold Medal Flour
½ cup brown sugar (packed)	2 tsp. baking powder
½ cup granulated sugar	½ tsp. salt
1 egg	1½ to 2 cups flaked coconut
	toasted whole almonds

Cook apricots in water over low heat 5 to 10 min. (water should be absorbed). Cool. Mix shortening and sugars until fluffy. Add egg, flavorings, and apricots. Measure flour by dipping method (p. 5) or by sifting. Mix flour, baking powder, and salt; stir in. Chill dough several hours.

Heat oven to 350° (mod.). Drop heaping teaspoonfuls of dough into coconut to coat. Place 2" apart on lightly greased baking sheet. Top with an almond. Bake 12 to 15 min. *Makes 6 doz. cookies.*

Note: *If you use Gold Medal Self-Rising Flour, omit baking powder and salt.*

LEMON CRINKLES

From Mrs. Alfred T. Neilsen of Council Bluffs, Iowa, who prefers simple and easy recipes that leave her time for her hobby of making hats.

½ cup shortening	1½ cups Gold Medal Flour
1 cup brown sugar (packed)	½ tsp. soda
1 egg	½ tsp. cream of tartar
about 1 tbsp. grated lemon rind	¼ tsp. salt
	¼ tsp. ginger
	granulated sugar

Heat oven to 350° (mod.). Mix shortening, sugar, and egg thoroughly; blend in lemon rind. Measure flour by dipping method (p. 5) or by sifting. Blend dry ingredients; stir into sugar mixture. Roll in 1" balls; dip tops in granulated sugar. Bake on ungreased baking sheet 10 to 12 min. *Makes about 3 doz. cookies.*

Note: *If you use Gold Medal Self-Rising Flour, omit soda and salt.*

COCONUT LEMON BARS

2 cups Gold Medal Flour	½ tsp. salt
½ cup butter or margarine	1 cup finely shredded coconut
¼ cup brown sugar (packed)	½ cup raisins
3 eggs, well beaten	½ cup walnuts, chopped
2 cups brown sugar (packed)	2 tbsp. lemon juice
	1 tsp. grated lemon rind

Heat oven to 350° (mod.). Measure flour by dipping method (p. 5) or by sifting. Mix flour, butter, and ¼ cup sugar thoroughly. Press firmly into bottom of a lightly greased oblong pan, 13x9½x2″. Bake 10 min.

Mix eggs, 2 cups sugar, and salt together thoroughly. Stir in rest of ingredients. Spread evenly over the partially baked bottom layer. Bake about 25 min. Top will be lightly browned. Cut in 3x1″ bars when cool. *Makes 28 bars.*

Note: *If you use Gold Medal Self-Rising Flour, omit salt.*

MONTEGO BAY SQUARES

1½ cups cut-up dates	½ cup brown sugar (packed)
2 tbsp. granulated sugar	¾ cup Gold Medal Flour
¾ cup water	¼ tsp. soda
½ sq. unsweetened chocolate (½ oz.)	½ tsp. salt
⅓ cup shortening (part butter or margarine)	¾ cup rolled oats
	⅓ cup chopped nuts

Heat oven to 400° (mod. hot). Grease a square pan, 8x8x2″. Cook dates, sugar, water, and chocolate over low heat, stirring constantly, until mixture thickens, about 10 min. Cool. Cream shortening and brown sugar thoroughly. Measure flour by dipping method (p. 5) or by sifting. Mix flour, soda, and salt; stir in. Mix in rolled oats and nuts. Press half of mixture over bottom of pan. Spread with date mixture; top with remaining crumbly mixture, pressing top lightly. Bake 25 to 30 min., or until golden brown. *Makes about 2 doz. bars.*

Note: *Increase chocolate in date mixture to 1 sq. (1 oz.) for more pronounced chocolate flavor.*

COCONUT BELLES

Since this cooky is better the second day than the day it is baked, you must bake them yesterday to enjoy them today.

½ cup shortening (part butter or margarine)	1 cup Gold Medal Flour
1 cup brown sugar (packed)	½ tsp. salt
1 egg	2 tsp. baking powder
½ tsp. vanilla	⅓ cup shredded coconut
¼ tsp. lemon extract	2 tbsp. finely chopped candied orange peel
2 tbsp. milk	

Heat oven to 325° (slow mod.). Mix shortening, sugar, egg, vanilla, lemon extract, and milk thoroughly. Measure flour by dipping method (p. 5) or by sifting. Mix flour, salt, and baking powder; stir in. Blend in coconut and peel. Spread in lightly greased square pan, 9x9x1¾″. Bake 30 to 35 min., or until golden brown. While warm, cut into 1½x1″ bars. Serve cool. *Makes 4 doz. bars.*

Note: *If you use Gold Medal Self-Rising Flour, omit salt and baking powder.*

BANANA OATMEAL COOKIES

¾ cup shortening
1 cup sugar
1 egg, beaten
1½ cups Gold Medal
    Flour
½ tsp. soda
1 tsp. salt
1 tsp. cinnamon
¼ tsp. nutmeg
1¾ cups rolled oats
1 cup mashed ripe
    bananas (2 to 3
    medium)
½ cup chopped nuts or
    raisins

Heat oven to 400° (mod. hot). Measure flour by dipping method (p. 5) or by sifting. Place all ingredients in mixing bowl. Beat until well blended. Drop rounded teaspoonfuls of dough about 1½″ apart on ungreased baking sheet. Bake 12 to 15 min. *Makes 4 doz. cookies.*

Note: *If you use Gold Medal Self-Rising Flour, omit soda and salt.*

BANANA-CHOCOLATE CHIP COOKIES

Make Banana Oatmeal Cookies (above)—except use ½ cup chocolate pieces instead of nuts or raisins.

HIDDEN CHOCOLATE COOKIES

½ cup shortening (part
    butter or
    margarine)
½ cup granulated
    sugar
¼ cup brown sugar
    (packed)
1 egg
1 tbsp. water
½ tsp. vanilla
1½ cups plus 2 tbsp.
    Gold Medal Flour
½ tsp. soda
¼ tsp. salt
about 3 doz. chocolate
    mint wafers

Mix thoroughly shortening, sugars, and egg. Stir in water and vanilla. Measure flour by dipping method (p. 5) or by sifting. Blend flour, soda, and salt; stir in. Chill dough.

   Heat oven to 400° (mod. hot). Shape cookies by enclosing each chocolate mint wafer in about 1 tbsp. dough. Place about 2″ apart on greased baking sheet. Bake 8 to 10 min., or until no imprint remains when touched lightly. *Makes about 3 doz. cookies.*

Note: *If you use Gold Medal Self-Rising Flour, omit soda and salt.*

JEWELED BARS

A chewy, moist bar with the added fun of candied orange slices. It contains no shortening but is rich in egg. "Perfect with a glass of cold milk," says Margret Johnson, who brought the recipe to us.

4 eggs, separated
2¼ cups brown sugar
    (packed)
1 tbsp. water
1 tsp. vanilla
2 cups Gold Medal
    Flour
1 tsp. baking powder
½ tsp. salt
1 cup candied orange
    slices (about 18),
    finely cut
¾ cup chopped
    walnuts

Heat oven to 350° (mod.). Beat egg yolks; add sugar, water, and vanilla. Measure flour by dipping method (p. 5) or by sifting. Blend dry ingredients; stir in. Mix in orange pieces and walnuts. Beat egg whites until stiff but not dry; stir in. Spread in well-greased oblong pan, 13x9½x2″. Bake 30 to 35 min. Cut in bars while warm. *Makes about 3 doz. bars.*

Note: *If you use Gold Medal Self-Rising Flour, omit baking powder and salt.*

JEWELED GUMDROP BARS

Make Jeweled Bars (above)—except use 1 cup multicolored gumdrops, finely cut, in place of orange slices.

RAISIN OATMEAL DROP COOKIES

Hearty and homey.

enough of our mashed
   Potato Buds for
   2 servings
½ cup shortening
1 cup granulated sugar
½ cup brown sugar
   (packed)
2 eggs
¼ cup soured milk
1½ cups Gold Medal
   Flour

1 tsp. salt
1 tsp. baking powder
¼ tsp. soda
1 tsp. cinnamon
½ tsp. nutmeg
½ tsp. cloves
1 cup raisins
½ cup chopped nuts
1½ cups quick-cooking
   rolled oats

Heat oven to 375° (quick mod.). Prepare potatoes as directed on pkg. for 2 servings (1 cup); set aside. Cream shortening and sugars. Add eggs and beat until light. Blend in milk and potatoes. Measure flour by dipping method (p. 5) or by sifting. Blend flour, salt, baking powder, soda, and spices; stir in. Fold in raisins, nuts, and rolled oats. Drop rounded teaspoonfuls of dough on lightly greased baking sheet. Bake 12 to 15 min. Store in airtight container. *Makes 5 doz. cookies.*

Note: *If you use Gold Medal Self-Rising Flour, omit salt and soda.*

HOW TO SOUR MILK OR CREAM

For ¼ cup: place 1 tsp. vinegar or lemon juice in cup measure, add milk or cream to ¼ cup level; let stand a few minutes before using. For 1 cup: use 1 tbsp. vinegar or lemon juice, add milk or cream to 1 cup level; let stand at room temperature 1 to 2 hr.

FILLED MOLASSES COOKIES

½ cup shortening
½ cup brown sugar
   (packed)
1 egg
½ cup molasses
¼ cup soured milk
   or buttermilk
3 cups Gold Medal
   Flour
1 tsp. soda

½ tsp. salt
1 tsp. baking powder
1 tsp. cinnamon
¼ tsp. cloves
¼ tsp. nutmeg
¾ cup orange
   marmalade
cut-up dates, candied
   fruit, or raisins

Heat oven to 375° (quick mod.). Mix shortening, sugar, and egg thoroughly. Stir in molasses and milk. Measure flour by dipping method (p. 5) or by sifting. Blend dry ingredients; stir in. If dough is too soft to roll, chill. Roll dough, ⅓ at a time, as thin as possible (1/16″ thick) on floured board. Cut in 2″ rounds. Place ½ tsp. marmalade on half the rounds; cover with remaining rounds. Top each cooky with a piece of cut-up date or candied fruit or a raisin. Place on lightly greased baking sheet. Bake 10 to 12 min. *Makes 5 doz. 2″ cookies.*

Note: *If you use Gold Medal Self-Rising Flour, omit soda, salt, and baking powder.*

CANDY-TOPPED OATMEAL BARS

1 cup butter or
   margarine
½ cup brown sugar
   (packed)
½ cup granulated
   sugar
2 egg yolks

1 cup Gold Medal
   Flour
1 cup rolled oats
6 chocolate candy bars
   (1 oz. each)
2 tbsp. butter
½ cup chopped nuts

Heat oven to 350° (mod.). Mix 1 cup butter, sugars, and egg yolks thoroughly. Measure flour by dipping method (p. 5) or by sifting. Stir in flour and oats. Spread in greased and floured oblong pan, 13x9½x2″. Bake 20 to 25 min. Cool 10 min. Melt chocolate and 2 tbsp. butter over hot water; spread over cooled cooky layer. Sprinkle with nuts; cut in bars. *Makes 4 doz. bars.*

Note: *You may use Gold Medal Self-Rising Flour in this recipe.*

Recipes we know and use today came from 'round the world to the thirteen isolated colonies of America. Plain and hearty cookies were the gustatory pleasure of our pioneers. The homespun flavors of sour cream, maple sugar, butterscotch, and cinnamon are still among our favorites. And though our tastes may now be trained to prefer white sugar to molasses and our eyes to select a fancy frosted cooky rather than a simple oatmeal drop, these cookies of our forefathers have won an enduring place in our hearts.

JOE FROGGERS

Our adaptation of the famous molasses cookies made long ago by old Uncle Joe of Marblehead, Mass. The cookies are as plump and dark as the little frogs that lived in the pond near Joe's cottage.

½ cup shortening	1½ tsp. salt
1 cup sugar	1 tsp. soda
1 cup dark molasses	1½ tsp. ginger
½ cup water	½ tsp. cloves
4 cups Gold Medal	½ tsp. nutmeg
Flour	¼ tsp. allspice

Mix well shortening and sugar. Stir in molasses and water. Measure flour by dipping method (p. 5) or by sifting. Stir dry ingredients together; blend into shortening mixture. Chill dough several hours or overnight.

Heat oven to 375° (quick mod.). Roll dough ¼" thick on floured board. Cut in 3" circles. Sprinkle with sugar. Place on well-greased baking sheet. Bake 10 to 12 min. Leave on baking sheet a few min. before removing to prevent breaking. Store in covered cooky jar. *Makes 3 to 4 doz. cookies.*

Note: *If you use Gold Medal Self-Rising Flour, omit salt and soda.*

ICE CREAM SANDWICHES

Slice round bulk ice cream; place slice between two Froggers (above). Or Froggers may be cut and baked as rectangles to be used with brick ice cream. After ice cream sandwiches are made, place in freezing compartment for at least an hour before serving.

SESAME SEED COOKIES

A modern-day version of early American Seed Cakes. For the original cooky, colonial mothers rolled cardamom, coriander, caraway, or sesame seeds into the rich dough.

½ cup butter or	2 cups Gold Medal
margarine	Flour
⅓ cup sesame seeds	1 tsp. baking powder
½ cup butter	¼ tsp. salt
1 cup sugar	Browned Butter Sesame
1 egg	Icing (below)
2 tbsp. water	

Heat oven to 375° (quick mod.). Brown ½ cup butter and sesame seeds in medium saucepan over low heat until golden brown (watch carefully to avoid burning); remove from heat. Mix ½ cup butter, sugar, and egg thoroughly. Add 2 tbsp. sesame seeds (from the browned butter) to sugar mixture. Blend in water.

Measure flour by dipping method (p. 5) or by sifting. Stir dry ingredients together; blend into sugar mixture. Drop dough by teaspoonfuls on ungreased baking sheet; flatten with bottom of greased glass dipped in sugar. Bake about 10 min., or until lightly browned around the edges. Cool and frost. *Makes 4 to 5 doz. cookies.*

Note: *If you use Gold Medal Self-Rising Flour, omit baking powder and salt.*

Browned Butter Sesame Icing: Blend 3 cups sifted confectioners' sugar, 3 tbsp. milk, and 1 tsp. vanilla into remainder of browned butter-sesame seed mixture. Stir until smooth.

JAN HAGEL

From Holland come these crisp, buttery-rich strips with baked-on nut glaze. Quick and easy, especially nice for teas or as an accompaniment to ice cream desserts. We call them Dutch Hail. See color picture opposite.

1 cup butter or
  margarine
1 cup sugar
1 egg, separated
2 cups Gold Medal
  Flour
½ tsp. cinnamon
1 tbsp. water
½ cup very finely
  chopped walnuts

Heat oven to 350° (mod.). Lightly grease a jelly roll pan, 15½x10½x1″. Mix butter, sugar, and egg yolk. Measure flour by dipping method (p. 5) or by sifting. Blend flour and cinnamon; stir into butter mixture. Pat into pan. Beat water and egg white until frothy; brush over dough; sprinkle with nuts. Bake 20 to 25 min., or until very lightly browned. Cut immediately into finger-like strips. *Makes fifty 3x1″ strips.*

Note: *You may use Gold Medal Self-Rising Flour in this recipe.*

BUTTERSCOTCH LACE COOKIES

See color picture opposite.

1 cup butter or
  margarine, melted
1½ cups brown sugar
  (packed)
2¼ cups rolled oats
½ tsp. salt
1 tbsp. molasses, if
  desired
3 tbsp. flour
1 egg, slightly beaten
1 tsp. vanilla

Add sugar to butter; pour over rolled oats. Let stand at room temperature overnight so oats absorb butter.

Heat oven to 375° (quick mod.). Mix remaining ingredients into oats. Drop level teaspoonfuls of dough 2″ apart on heavily greased baking sheet. Bake only 12 cookies on a sheet. Bake 5 to 7 min., or until brown around edges. Allow to remain on sheet a few min. until firm, then immediately remove with spatula to cooling rack. *Makes 6 doz. cookies.*

Note: *Do not make these cookies in hot, humid weather, as cookies absorb moisture from air and become limp.*

FILLED OATMEAL COOKIES

See color picture opposite.

2 cups Gold Medal
  Flour
1 tsp. salt
½ tsp. soda
½ cup brown sugar
  (packed)
¾ cup shortening
1 egg
¼ cup molasses
1 cup rolled oats
Pumpkin Filling or
  Date Filling
  (below)

Heat oven to 375° (quick mod.). Measure flour by dipping method (p. 5) or by sifting. Blend flour, salt, and soda. Add sugar, shortening, egg, and molasses; stir until smooth. Blend in rolled oats. Roll dough out ⅛″ thick on lightly floured board. Cut with 2½″ round cutter. Place half the rounds on ungreased baking sheet. Spread 1 tsp. Filling lightly on center of each cooky. Cut a cross or other pattern on remaining rounds; place over filling-topped rounds. Seal edges. Bake 12 to 15 min. *Makes 2 doz. filled cookies.*

Note: *If you use Gold Medal Self-Rising Flour, omit salt and soda.*

Pumpkin Filling: Mix 1 cup cooked or canned pumpkin, ½ cup sugar, ½ tsp. cinnamon, ½ tsp. ginger, and ¼ tsp. nutmeg.

Date Filling: Boil together 1 cup cut-up pitted dates (about ½ lb.), ½ cup sugar, and ¼ cup water until thick, stirring constantly. Stir in ½ cup chopped nuts. Cool before using.

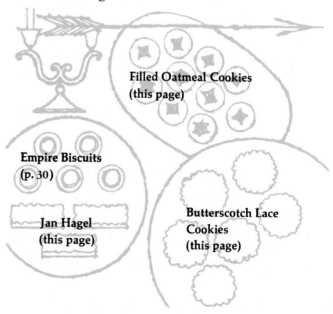

Filled Oatmeal Cookies
(this page)

Empire Biscuits
(p. 30)

Jan Hagel
(this page)

Butterscotch Lace
Cookies
(this page)

EMPIRE BISCUITS

Our easy-to-make version of a cooky popular in Williamsburg, Virginia, during the golden era when that lovely city was the social center of the Southern colonies. See color picture, p. 29.

Make dough for Vanilla Refrigerator Cookies (p. 53). Shape rolls 1½″ in diameter; slice thin and bake. Put two cooled cookies together with currant jelly as filling. Frost top cooky with Easy Creamy Icing (p. 60); decorate as desired.

STONE JAR MOLASSES COOKIES

Crisp and brown ... and so delicious.

1 cup light molasses	2¼ cups Gold Medal
½ cup shortening	Flour
1 tsp. soda	1¾ tsp. baking powder
	1 tsp. salt
	1½ tsp. ginger

Heat molasses to boiling point. Remove from heat. Stir in shortening and soda. Measure flour by dipping method (p. 5) or by sifting. Blend remaining ingredients together; stir in. Chill dough.

Heat oven to 350° (mod.). Roll dough out very thin (1/16″) on lightly floured board. Cut in desired shapes. Place on lightly greased baking sheet. Bake 5 to 7 min., or until set. Do not overbake! *Makes about 6 doz. 2½″ cookies.*

Note: *If you use Gold Medal Self-Rising Flour, omit soda, baking powder, and salt.*

CENTENNIAL MOLASSES SPICE DROPS

One hundred years ago homemakers used vinegar in much of their cooking—even in cooky baking.

⅔ cup shortening (part butter or margarine)	3 cups Gold Medal Flour
⅔ cup sugar	¾ tsp. soda
2 eggs	¼ tsp. salt
⅔ cup molasses	¾ tsp. cinnamon
	¾ tsp. ginger
	¼ cup cider vinegar

Heat oven to 375° (quick mod.). Mix shortening, sugar, eggs, and molasses thoroughly. Measure flour by dipping method (p. 5) or by sifting. Blend dry ingredients; add alternately with vinegar to batter. Mix well. Drop dough by teaspoonfuls about 2″ apart on lightly greased baking sheet. Bake 8 to 10 min., or until no imprint remains when touched lightly. *Makes 5 doz. cookies.*

Note: *If you use Gold Medal Self-Rising Flour, omit soda and salt.*

CHEWY MOLASSES COOKIES

A flat wafer-like cooky.

⅓ cup shortening	½ tsp. salt
½ cup sugar	½ tsp. cinnamon
2 eggs	¼ tsp. cloves
½ cup molasses	¼ tsp. allspice
2 tbsp. milk	1 cup currants
1¼ cups Gold Medal Flour	½ cup chopped nuts
1 tsp. soda	2 tsp. vanilla

Cream shortening and sugar thoroughly. Stir in eggs, molasses, and milk; blend well. Measure flour by dipping method (p. 5) or by sifting. Blend dry ingredients; stir in. Add currants, nuts, and vanilla. Mix well. Chill several hours or until firm.

Heat oven to 350° (mod.). Drop dough by small teaspoonfuls about 2″ apart on well-greased baking sheet. Bake about 15 min. Let baked cookies remain on baking sheet for a moment before removing. *Makes about 4 doz. 2½″ cookies.*

Note: *If you use Gold Medal Self-Rising Flour, omit soda and salt.*

HOW TO FRESHEN DROP COOKIES

Freshen drop cookies by reheating in a covered casserole in slow oven (300°) 8 to 10 min.; re-crisp cookies on an ungreased baking sheet or in a shallow pan in a slow oven (300°) 3 to 5 min.

BUTTERMILK COOKIES

½ cup shortening (part butter or margarine)	3 cups Gold Medal Flour
1 cup sugar	1 tsp. baking powder
1 egg	½ tsp. soda
½ cup buttermilk or soured milk (p. 26)	½ tsp. salt
2 tsp. vanilla	1 tsp. nutmeg
	¼ cup sugar
	1 tsp. cinnamon

Mix shortening, 1 cup sugar, and egg thoroughly. Stir in buttermilk and vanilla. Measure flour by dipping method (p. 5) or by sifting. Blend dry ingredients into shortening mixture. Chill dough 1 hr.

Heat oven to 400° (mod. hot). Drop by tablespoonfuls on greased baking sheet. Flatten with bottom of greased glass dipped in mixture of ¼ cup sugar and cinnamon. Bake 8 to 10 min. *Makes about 30 cookies.*

Note: *If you use Gold Medal Self-Rising Flour, omit baking powder, soda, and salt.*

SOUR CREAM-NUT COOKIES

Flavor of Grandma's sour cream rolled cookies with modern easy method of drop-and-flatten.

⅓ cup shortening	½ tsp. nutmeg
⅔ cup sugar	½ cup commercial sour cream
1 egg	
1⅔ cups Gold Medal Flour	½ cup finely chopped nuts
1 tsp. baking powder	1 tbsp. sugar
¼ tsp. soda	¼ tsp. nutmeg
½ tsp. salt	

Heat oven to 400° (mod. hot). Mix shortening, ⅔ cup sugar, and egg thoroughly. Measure flour by dipping method (p. 5) or by sifting. Stir dry ingredients together; blend into shortening-sugar mixture alternately with sour cream. Stir in nuts. Drop dough by teaspoonfuls about 2″ apart on greased baking sheet. Flatten with greased bottom of glass dipped in sugar. Mix 1 tbsp. sugar and nutmeg; sprinkle on top of cookies. Bake 8 to 10 min. *Makes about 3 doz. cookies.*

Note: *If you use Gold Medal Self-Rising Flour, omit baking powder, soda, and salt.*

BANANA JUMBOS

1 cup shortening (part butter or margarine)	½ cup buttermilk
	1 tsp. vanilla
	3 cups Gold Medal Flour
1 cup sugar	
2 eggs	1½ tsp. soda
1 cup mashed ripe bananas (2 to 3)	½ tsp. salt
	1 cup chopped nuts

Mix shortening, sugar, and eggs thoroughly. Stir in bananas, buttermilk, and vanilla. Measure flour by dipping method (p. 5) or by sifting. Stir flour, soda, and salt together; stir in. Blend in nuts. Chill 1 hr.

Heat oven to 375° (quick mod.). Drop rounded tablespoonfuls of dough 2″ apart on lightly greased baking sheet. Bake about 10 min., or until delicately browned. If desired, frost with a thin confectioners' sugar icing. *Makes about 3½ doz. cookies.*

Note: *If you use Gold Medal Self-Rising Flour, omit soda and salt.*

INDIAN JUMANAS

South American Indians use achiote, the seed of the annatto tree, to color these tender nutmeg-flavored cookies yellow, and chopped wild spinach for the green color. Food coloring is used for our version.

⅔ cup butter or margarine	2¾ cups Gold Medal Flour
1 cup sugar	1 tsp. soda
2 eggs	½ tsp. salt
1 tsp. vanilla	½ tsp. nutmeg
½ cup commercial sour cream	yellow and green food coloring
	raisins or nuts

Heat oven to 375° (quick mod.). Mix butter, sugar, eggs, and vanilla until fluffy; stir in sour cream. Measure flour by dipping method (p. 5) or by sifting. Blend dry ingredients; stir into butter mixture. Divide dough in two portions; color half yellow and half green. Drop dough by heaping teaspoonfuls on lightly greased baking sheet. Press raisin or nut meat into center of each cooky. Bake 8 to 10 min., or until lightly browned. *Makes 6 doz. cookies.*

Note: *If you use Gold Medal Self-Rising Flour, omit soda and salt.*

RHUBARB COCONUT COOKIES

Ask your family and friends to guess what gives this cooky its tangy flavor. A new idea for using leftover rhubarb sauce.

½ cup shortening	1 tsp. baking powder
¼ cup sugar	½ tsp. soda
¾ cup corn syrup	½ tsp. salt
1 egg	1 tsp. nutmeg
1 cup thick, cooked rhubarb	¼ tsp. cloves
	1 cup coconut
2 cups Gold Medal Flour	½ cup raisins
	½ cup chopped nuts

Heat oven to 375° (quick mod.). Mix shortening, sugar, syrup, egg, and rhubarb thoroughly. Measure flour by dipping method (p. 5) or by sifting. Blend flour, baking powder, soda, salt, nutmeg, and cloves. Blend rhubarb and flour mixture together. Stir in coconut, raisins, and chopped nuts. Drop dough by heaping teaspoonfuls on greased baking sheet. Bake 15 to 18 min. *Makes 5½ doz. cookies.*

Note: *If you use Gold Medal Self-Rising Flour, omit baking powder, soda, and salt.*

PEACH COCONUT COOKIES

Make Rhubarb Coconut Cookies (above)—except use 1¼ cups (1-lb. can) drained chopped peaches in place of rhubarb.

EASY CHINESE ALMOND COOKIES

Perfect accompaniment for Chinese dishes or holiday party foods.

1 cup Gold Medal Flour	½ tsp. almond extract or vanilla
½ cup shortening (half butter or margarine)	1 egg yolk
½ tsp. salt	1 tbsp. water
¼ cup plus 2 tbsp. sugar	¼ cup blanched almonds

Measure flour by dipping method (p. 5) or by sifting. Place flour in bowl. Cut in shortening. Work salt, sugar, and flavoring in with hands. Shape in long roll 1″ in diameter; wrap in waxed paper. Chill about 1 hr.

Heat oven to 400° (mod. hot). Cut dough in ¼″ slices. Place about 1″ apart on lightly greased baking sheet. Brush each cooky with a mixture of egg yolk and water. Press ½ blanched almond in top of each cooky. Bake 8 to 10 min., or until light golden brown. Allow cookies to cool slightly before removing from baking sheet so they won't crumble. *Makes about 2 doz. cookies.*

Note: *If you use Gold Medal Self-Rising Flour, omit salt.*

BROWN SUGAR PECAN ROUNDS

½ cup butter or margarine	1¼ cups Gold Medal Flour
1¼ cups brown sugar (packed)	¼ tsp. soda
1 egg	⅛ tsp. salt
	½ cup coarsely chopped pecans

Heat oven to 350° (mod.). Cream butter and brown sugar thoroughly. Beat egg in well. Measure flour by dipping method (p. 5) or by sifting. Stir dry ingredients together; blend in. Stir in pecans. Drop by ¼ teaspoonfuls about 2″ apart on greased baking sheet. (Cookies flatten and spread.) Bake 7 to 8 min. *Makes about 10 doz. 1½″ cookies.*

Note: *If you use Gold Medal Self-Rising Flour, omit soda and salt.*

CHOCOLATE OATMEAL REFRIGERATOR COOKIES

Pleasing combination . . . oatmeal gives a delightful coconut quality.

½ cup shortening	2 sq. unsweetened chocolate (2 oz.), melted
1 cup brown sugar (packed)	
1 egg	1 cup Gold Medal Flour
1 tsp. vanilla	½ tsp. soda
½ tsp. almond extract	½ tsp. salt
	1 cup rolled oats
	½ cup chopped nuts

Mix shortening, sugar, egg, and flavorings thoroughly. Blend in chocolate. Measure flour by dipping method (p. 5) or by sifting. Stir dry ingredients together; blend in. Stir in rolled oats and nuts. Mold in roll 1½″ in diameter. Wrap in waxed paper. Chill thoroughly several hours or overnight.

Heat oven to 350° (mod.). Slice dough ¼″ thick using a thin, very sharp knife. Place about 1″ apart on ungreased baking sheet. Bake 10 to 12 min. *Makes about 4 doz. cookies.*

Note: *If you use Gold Medal Self-Rising Flour, omit soda and salt.*

CHOCOLATE OATMEAL BONBONS

Make Chocolate Oatmeal Refrigerator Cookies (above)—except shape dough in 1″ balls. Bake in 350° (mod.) oven 12 min. *Makes 5½ doz. bonbons.*

DELTA BARS

Nutty brown sugar meringue bakes into cooky base to make chewy butterscotch bar. Popular with young and old.

½ cup shortening	1 tsp. baking powder
1 cup granulated sugar	½ tsp. salt
1 whole egg	1 cup brown sugar
1 egg, separated	(packed)
1 tsp. vanilla	½ cup chopped nuts
1¼ cups Gold Medal	
Flour	

Heat oven to 375° (quick mod.). Mix shortening, granulated sugar, egg, egg yolk, and vanilla well. Measure flour by dipping method (p. 5) or by sifting. Stir dry ingredients together; blend into shortening mixture. Mix thoroughly. Spread in greased oblong pan, 13x9½x2". Beat egg white until foamy. Gradually beat in brown sugar. Continue beating until mixture is stiff and glossy. Fold in nuts. Spread meringue over dough in pan. Bake about 25 min. Cut while warm in 2" squares. *Makes 2 doz. cookies.*

Note: *If you use Gold Medal Self-Rising Flour, omit baking powder and salt.*

CHOCOLATE LOGS

½ cup shortening (all	2 sq. unsweetened
or part butter or	chocolate (2 oz.)
margarine)	melted
1 cup sugar	½ tsp. salt
1 egg	¾ cup nuts, finely
2 tsp. vanilla	chopped
2 cups Gold Medal	
Flour	

Mix shortening, sugar, egg, and vanilla thoroughly. Measure flour by dipping method (p. 5) or by sifting. Stir flour, chocolate, and salt into shortening mixture. Mix in nuts. Shape mixture in rectangle, 12x8", on well-greased baking sheet. Cover with waxed paper; chill until firm.

Heat oven to 375° (quick mod.). Cut in 48 logs, 4x½". Place a little apart on ungreased baking sheet. Bake 10 to 12 min. *Makes 4 doz. logs.*

Note: *If you use Gold Medal Self-Rising Flour, omit salt.*

HIS MOTHER'S OATMEAL COOKIES

2 cups Gold Medal	1 cup shortening (part
Flour	butter or
1 tsp. soda	margarine)
½ tsp. salt	⅓ cup milk or soured
3 cups rolled oats	milk
	1½ cups brown sugar
	(packed)
	jelly or jam

Measure flour by dipping method (p. 5) or by sifting. Mix flour, soda, salt, and rolled oats. Cut in shortening until mixture is well blended. Stir in milk and sugar. Chill.

Heat oven to 375° (quick mod.). Roll dough ⅛" thick on lightly floured board. Cut in desired shapes. Place on ungreased baking sheet. Bake 10 to 12 min., or until lightly browned. When cool, and just before serving, put together in pairs with jelly or jam between. *Makes about 4 doz. 2½" double cookies.*

Note: *If you use Gold Medal Self-Rising Flour, omit soda and salt.*

Company Best Cookies

"Company is coming" is a magic phrase which brings an air of excitement to the house, especially to the kitchen. Often it is these company occasions that prompt us to take the time and effort to bake some delicious delicacy. Here, for the four o'clock hostess, are dainty bars, bonbons, and drops—perfect complements to fragrant tea or coffee. Among these teatime treasures you'll find cookies with the distinctive flavors and shapes of foreign lands. Here, too, for hostesses at big affairs, is a variety of cookies to make in quantity. Yes, cookies lend themselves beautifully to easy friendly hospitality. Baked, and even arranged ahead of time, cookies can always be ready to tempt and please your guests.

Afternoon tea is a gracious and elegant way to entertain your friends with ease and at a small expense. Welcome a newcomer to the neighborhood or honor an out-of-town guest at a small tea for twelve. Announce your daughter's engagement or introduce prospective club members at a large tea for fifty or one hundred guests. On these pages are dozens of recipes for fancy, rich, and delicious little cookies to accompany tea and coffee.

CHEESE DAINTIES

A rich, flaky cream cheese cooky with filling of your favorite preserves.

1 cup Gold Medal Flour	**¼ cup plus 2 tbsp.**
½ cup butter or marga-	**thick preserves,**
rine (¼ lb.)	**such as cherry**
4 oz. cream cheese	**1 egg white, beaten until**
(½ of 8-oz. pkg.)	**frothy**
	granulated sugar

Measure flour by dipping method (p. 5) or by sifting. Cut butter and cheese into flour until particles are size of giant peas. Work dough with hands until it cleans bowl; press firmly into ball. Chill about 1 hr.

Heat oven to 375° (quick mod.). Flatten dough with hand; roll 1/16″ thick on floured board. Cut in 5x2½″ rectangles; spread with 1 level tsp. of preserves, leaving ½″ at edges. Roll up carefully, beginning at narrow side. Seal well by pinching edge of dough into roll. Place pinched edge underneath on ungreased baking sheet; press down lightly. Brush with egg white; sprinkle generously with sugar. Bake about 15 min., or until slightly browned on top. *Makes about 18 dainties.*

Note: *Do not use Gold Medal Self-Rising Flour in this recipe.*

CHEESE TRIANGLES

Make Cheese Dainties (above)—except cut in 2″ squares with knife or pastry wheel. Place ¼ tsp. preserves in center of each square. Fold over, forming triangles; seal edges with fingers or tines of fork. *Makes 3 doz. triangles.*

ALMOND MERINGUE SHORTBREADS

2 cups Gold Medal	**½ cup jam or jelly**
Flour	**2 egg whites**
2 egg yolks	**½ cup sugar**
½ cup sugar	**¼ tsp. cinnamon**
¼ tsp. salt	**½ cup slivered**
¾ cup butter or	**blanched almonds**
margarine	

Heat oven to 400° (mod. hot). Measure flour by dipping method (p. 5) or by sifting. Make a well in center of flour; add egg yolks, ½ cup sugar, salt, and butter. Work together with hands until well blended. Press dough into ungreased square pan, 9x9x1¾″. Bake 15 to 20 min. Cool slightly; spread with jam or jelly. Beat egg whites until foamy. Gradually add ½ cup sugar and cinnamon. Continue beating until egg whites stand in stiff peaks. Spread meringue over jam; sprinkle with almonds. Bake 8 to 10 min., or until meringue is brown. Cut in 1½″ squares. *Makes 3 doz. squares.*

Note: *If you use Gold Medal Self-Rising Flour, omit salt.*

CHEESE SWIRL BROWNIES

Golden filling marbled into a delightful cake-like brownie. Developed by Marcia McMullen of Ohio State University while working in our kitchens on a special student project.

Heat oven to 375° (quick mod.). Spread half the Brownie Dough (below) in greased square pan, 9x9x 1¾"; pour Cheese Mixture (below) over. Spread remaining Brownie Dough over top. Pull knife through in both directions to marble. Bake 40 to 45 min., or until toothpick stuck in center comes out clean. Cool; cut in squares. *Makes 3 doz. 1½" squares.*

Brownie Dough

1 cup sugar	1 cup Softasilk Cake
½ cup butter or	Flour
margarine	½ tsp. baking powder
2 eggs	½ tsp. salt
½ tsp. vanilla	1 cup chopped walnuts
2 sq. unsweetened	
chocolate (2 oz.),	
melted	

Mix sugar, butter, eggs, and vanilla. Blend in chocolate. Measure flour by spooning into cup and leveling off or by sifting. Blend rest of ingredients thoroughly; mix into chocolate mixture.

Cheese Mixture

¼ cup sugar	1 tbsp. cornstarch
2 tbsp. butter	1 egg
1 cup cream-style	½ tsp. vanilla
cottage cheese	

Cream sugar and butter. Add cottage cheese and cornstarch; mix thoroughly. Add egg and vanilla; blend well, using electric mixer or rotary beater.

NUT BONBON COOKIES

1 pkg. (8 oz.) cream	2 cups Gold Medal
cheese	Flour
1 cup shortening (part	confectioners' sugar
butter or	9 doz. walnut halves
margarine)	

Mix cheese and shortening with fork. Measure flour by dipping method (p. 5) or by sifting. Mix flour in well with hands. Chill several hours or overnight.

Heat oven to 375° (quick mod.). Roll out ⅛" thick on cloth-covered board sprinkled with confectioners' sugar. (This amount of dough will absorb about 1 cup confectioners' sugar.) Cut dough in oblongs, 3x1". Put a walnut half on each oblong; roll up. Place on baking sheet with end of roll underneath. Bake 15 to 17 min., or until golden brown. Sprinkle cookies immediately with confectioners' sugar. Serve warm if possible. Prunes, raisins, maraschino cherries, finely shredded coconut, pecans, etc. may be substituted for walnuts. *Makes 9 doz. cookies.*

Note: *You may use Gold Medal Self-Rising Flour in this recipe.*

APRICOT COCONUT TARTLETS

½ cup shortening (all	¼ tsp. salt
or part butter or	1 cup Gold Medal
margarine)	Flour
1 pkg. (3 oz.) cream	apricot jam
cheese	¼ cup flaked coconut
1 tsp. sugar	

Mix shortening, cream cheese, sugar, and salt thoroughly. Measure flour by dipping method (p. 5) or by sifting. Blend flour into shortening mixture. Form dough into a ball; chill at least 3 hr. (If desired, dough may be refrigerated about 1 week.)

Heat oven to 400° (mod. hot). Roll dough out ⅛" thick on lightly floured cloth-covered board. Cut with 2" cooky cutter; place on ungreased baking sheet. Top each round with ½ tsp. apricot jam. Bake about 10 min. Remove from oven; quickly sprinkle each tartlet with coconut. Bake 2 min. more, or until tartlets are delicately browned. Remove from baking sheet. Cool. *Makes about 3½ doz. tartlets.*

Note: *Do not use Gold Medal Self-Rising Flour in this recipe.*

FLORENTINES

Developed after Helen Hallbert, our former director, returned from Europe singing the praises of this luscious chocolate-orange cooky. See color picture opposite.

¾ cup whipping cream (35% butterfat)

¼ cup sugar

¼ cup Gold Medal Flour

½ cup slivered almonds (blanched or toasted), very finely chopped

½ lb. candied orange peel, very finely chopped

2 bars (4 oz. each) German sweet chocolate

Heat oven to 350° (mod.). Stir cream and sugar together until well blended. Stir in flour, almonds, and orange peel. Drop dough by scant teaspoonfuls on heavily greased and floured baking sheet. Flatten cooky with knife or spatula. Bake 10 to 12 min., or just until cookies brown lightly around edges. Leave cookies on baking sheet for few min. to firm up. Melt chocolate bars over hot water. Turn cookies upside down; spread with chocolate. Allow to dry several hours or overnight at room temperature until chocolate becomes firm. Store in covered container or in refrigerator. *Makes 5 doz. cookies.*

SPANISH ANISE STICKS

2 cups Gold Medal Flour

1 tsp. baking powder

¼ tsp. salt

¾ cup sugar

¼ cup shortening

2 eggs, well beaten

2 drops anise oil

Heat oven to 375° (quick mod.). Measure flour by dipping method (p. 5) or by sifting. Blend dry ingredients; cut in shortening until particles are size of large peas. Stir in eggs and anise oil; mix thoroughly with hands. Using ½ dough at a time, roll ¼" thick on lightly floured board. Cut in sticks, 4x½". Place on ungreased baking sheet, about ½" apart. Brush with soft or melted butter or margarine. Bake 10 to 12 min. *Makes 3 to 4 doz. cookies.*

Note: *If you use Gold Medal Self-Rising Flour, omit baking powder and salt.*

GÂTEAU BONBONS

Tiny frosted filled cookies from France. This recipe, together with many others from foreign lands, was shared with us by Loyta Higgins of our staff, who has lived all over the world. See color picture opposite.

⅔ cup soft butter or margarine

1 cup sugar

1 egg

1 pkg. (3 oz.) cream cheese, softened

½ tsp. lemon juice

1 tsp. finely grated lemon rind

2 cups Gold Medal Flour

½ tsp. baking powder

½ tsp. salt

⅛ tsp. soda

orange marmalade

Easy Creamy Icing (p. 60)

Mix first 6 ingredients until light and fluffy. Measure flour by dipping method (p. 5) or by sifting. Blend dry ingredients; add to butter mixture; mix well. Chill.

Heat oven to 350° (mod.). Using ¼ of dough at a time (keep rest refrigerated), roll ⅛" thick on lightly floured board. Cut 1" rounds. Place half the rounds on lightly greased baking sheet. Put ¼ tsp. marmalade in center of each. (For larger bonbons: cut 1½" rounds; fill with ½ tsp. marmalade.) Cover with remaining half of rounds; seal edges with floured finger. Bake 8 to 10 min., or until edges are slightly browned. When cool, frost with tinted Icing. *Makes 7 doz. 1" bonbons.*

Note: *Do not use Gold Medal Self-Rising Flour in this recipe.*

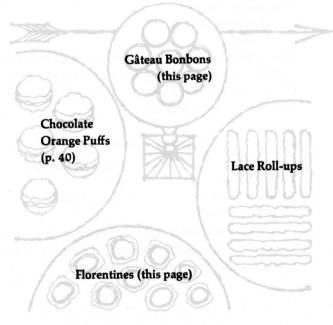

Gâteau Bonbons (this page)

Chocolate Orange Puffs (p. 40)

Lace Roll-ups

Florentines (this page)

CHOCOLATE ORANGE PUFFS

Orange-flavored miniature cream puffs filled with chocolate cream. See color picture, p. 39.

½ cup water
¼ cup butter or
    margarine
⅛ tsp. salt
½ cup Gold Medal
    Flour

2 eggs
grated rind of 1 orange
    (2 to 3 tbsp.)
Chocolate Cream
    Filling (below)

Heat oven to 450° (hot). Blend water, butter, and salt; bring to a boil. Measure flour by dipping method (p. 5) or by sifting. Add flour; stir briskly until mixture leaves the pan and forms a smooth ball, about 1 min. Remove from heat; add one egg at a time; beat well after each addition. Fold in orange rind. Drop dough by level teaspoonfuls on ungreased baking sheet. Bake 12 to 15 min. Remove from baking sheet immediately; cool. Fill with Filling. Refrigerate until served. *Makes 4 to 5 doz. puffs.*

Note: *If you use Gold Medal Self-Rising Flour, omit salt.*

Chocolate Cream Filling: Melt ½ cup semi-sweet chocolate pieces over hot (not boiling) water. Add 2 tbsp. orange juice or water. Remove from heat and cool. Fold in ⅓ cup finely chopped almonds. Beat ½ cup whipping cream until stiff. Fold into chocolate mixture.

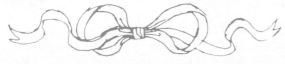

ALMOND BUTTER COOKIES

1 cup butter
½ cup sugar
1 cup finely chopped
    almonds (don't
    remove skins)

2 tsp. vanilla
2 cups Gold Medal Flour

Heat oven to 350° (mod.). Cream butter and sugar together. Stir in almonds and vanilla. Measure flour by dipping method (p. 5) or by sifting. Blend in flour with pastry blender. Form in small balls (scant teaspoonfuls). Place on ungreased baking sheet. Flatten with bottom of greased glass dipped in sugar. Bake 9 to 10 min., or until slightly browned. *Makes about 6 doz. cookies.*

PARISIAN ORANGE COOKIES

This unusual cooky is crisp like a sugar cooky, yet has a chewy confection-like quality.

2 tbsp. coarsely grated
    orange rind
½ cup water
¼ cup sugar
½ cup butter or
    margarine

1 cup sugar
1 tbsp. sherry flavoring
1¼ cups Gold Medal
    Flour
1 tbsp. baking powder
½ tsp. salt

Heat oven to 375° (quick mod.). Blend orange rind, water, and ¼ cup sugar in saucepan; boil gently over med. heat 10 to 15 min., until mixture is thin syrup consistency. Add enough water to make ¼ cup syrup. Cream butter, 1 cup sugar, and flavoring until fluffy. Measure flour by dipping method (p. 5) or by sifting; blend dry ingredients. Stir syrup, then dry ingredients into creamed mixture; mix thoroughly. Roll in 1" balls. Place 2" apart on lightly greased baking sheet. Flatten with bottom of greased glass dipped in sugar. Bake about 8 min. *Makes 4½ doz. cookies.*

Note: *If you use Gold Medal Self-Rising Flour, omit baking powder and salt.*

CHOCOLATE WAFERS

1 sq. unsweetened
    chocolate (1 oz.)
½ cup shortening
    (half butter or
    margarine)
½ cup sugar
1 egg

¼ tsp. vanilla
¼ cup Gold Medal
    Flour
¼ tsp. salt
⅓ cup finely chopped
    nuts

Heat oven to 375° (quick mod.). Melt chocolate and shortening together over hot water. Remove from heat; beat in sugar, egg, and vanilla; blend well. Mix in flour and salt. Spread in well-greased jelly roll pan, 15½x10½x1". Sprinkle with nuts. Bake 15 min. Do not cool. Cut in 2½x1" strips; immediately remove from pan. *Makes 7½ doz. strips.*

Note: *If cookies harden in pan before all are removed, place pan in oven a few minutes to soften them.*

CHOCOLATE TRIANGLES

Make Chocolate Wafers (above)—except cut in 2" squares, cutting each square into a triangle.

KOULOURIA

From Smyrna. See color picture at left.

½ cup butter	1½ cups Gold Medal
½ cup sugar	Flour
1 whole egg	½ tsp. soda
1 egg, separated	½ tsp. salt
1½ tsp. vanilla	¼ cup sugar

Mix butter, ½ cup sugar, 1 whole egg, 1 egg yolk (reserve the egg white), and vanilla until light and fluffy. Measure flour by dipping method (p. 5) or by sifting. Stir flour, soda, and salt together; blend into butter mixture, kneading to a stiff dough. Chill 2 hr.

Heat oven to 350° (mod.). Shape heaping teaspoonfuls of dough into pencil-like strips (6″ long and ¼″ thick) by rolling under fingers on floured board. Form in double twist on greased baking sheet (as pictured). Beat reserved egg white with ¼ cup sugar until frothy; brush tops of cookies with this mixture. Bake 15 min. *Makes 4 doz. cookies.*

Note: *If you use Gold Medal Self-Rising Flour, omit soda and salt.*

BUTTER HORN COOKIES

See color picture at left.

2 cups Gold Medal	2 eggs, separated
Flour	¼ cup commercial
1 tsp. baking powder	sour cream
¼ tsp. salt	½ tsp. vanilla
½ cup butter	½ cup granulated sugar
½ pkg. active dry	½ cup finely ground
yeast (1½ tsp.)	walnuts or pecans
2 tbsp. warm water	½ tsp. almond extract
	confectioners' sugar

Measure flour by dipping method (p. 5) or by sifting. Stir flour, baking powder, and salt together in mixing bowl. Cut in butter. Dissolve yeast in water; stir in egg yolks, sour cream, and vanilla. Blend into flour mixture. Refrigerate 1 hr.

Heat oven to 400° (mod. hot). Beat egg whites until foamy; gradually add sugar; beat until stiff. Fold in nuts and almond extract. Divide dough in 4 parts. Roll each part into 9″ circle on board sprinkled with confectioners' sugar. Cut each circle in 12 wedges. Spread 1 heaping teaspoonful meringue on each. Roll, beginning at wide end. Bake on lightly greased baking sheet 10 to 12 min., or until golden brown. Sprinkle with confectioners' sugar. *Makes 4 doz. cookies.*

Note: *Do not use Gold Medal Self-Rising Flour in this recipe.*

TINY FUDGE TARTS

See color picture at right.

1½ cups Gold Medal Flour	3 tbsp. water
¼ tsp. salt	1 tsp. vanilla
½ cup butter or margarine	Fudge Filling (below)

Heat oven to 350° (mod.). Measure flour by dipping method (p. 5) or by sifting. Mix flour and salt; cut in butter. Sprinkle with water and vanilla; mix well with fork. Using ½ of dough at a time, roll out 1/16″ thick on cloth-covered board generously sprinkled with sugar. Cut in 2½″ squares. Spread 1 level tsp. Filling in center of each square. Bring corners to center; seal together. Place sealed side up or down on ungreased baking sheet. Bake 15 to 20 min. *Makes about 2½ doz. tarts.*

Note: *If you use Gold Medal Self-Rising Flour, omit salt.*

Fudge Filling: Mix the following ingredients thoroughly: ¼ cup butter or margarine, 1 egg yolk, ½ cup sugar, 1 tsp. vanilla, ¼ cup cocoa, and ½ cup finely chopped nuts or flaked coconut.

CHOCOLATE-COCONUT CANDIES

From Marie Thorn. See color picture at right.

¾ cup mashed potatoes (homemade or made from our mashed Potato Buds)	1 lb. confectioners' sugar (about 4¾ cups, sifted)
1 lb. flaked coconut (about 4 cups)	1 tsp. almond extract Chocolate Coating (below)

Combine ingredients except Coating; drop by heaping teaspoonfuls on waxed paper. Roll in balls; refrigerate ½ to 1 hr. If mixture is too soft to form balls, refrigerate first, then shape balls. Dip balls in Coating, turning to coat on all sides. Keep chocolate over hot water while dipping candy. With tongs or forks, lift balls out of chocolate on waxed paper or cake rack. Place candies in refrigerator to harden. *Makes about 5 doz. candies.*

Chocolate Coating: Mix 2 tbsp. soft butter, 2 tbsp. corn syrup, and 3 tbsp. water in the top of a double boiler. Stir in 1 pkg. of our chocolate fudge flavor frosting mix until smooth. Heat over rapidly boiling water 5 min., stirring occasionally.

Food plans for large affairs, such as receptions, church luncheons, teas, and club meetings, often call for hundreds of cookies. If you have been asked to be responsible for baking cookies for such an affair, these easy-to-make, easy-to-multiply cookies are just what you're looking for.

ORANGE PECAN COOKIES

Ingredients for 5 doz.	Ingredients for 10 doz.
½ cup shortening (part butter or margarine)	1 cup shortening (part butter or margarine)
1 cup brown sugar (packed)	2 cups brown sugar (packed)
1 egg	2 eggs
1 tbsp. grated orange rind	2 tbsp. grated orange rind
½ tsp. vanilla	1 tsp. vanilla
1¾ cups Gold Medal Flour	3½ cups Gold Medal Flour
¼ tsp. salt	½ tsp. salt
½ tsp. soda	1 tsp. soda
½ cup chopped pecans	1 cup chopped pecans

Mix shortening, sugar, egg(s), rind, and vanilla. Measure flour by dipping method (p. 5) or by sifting. Blend flour, salt, and soda; stir in. Stir in pecans. Form into rolls 2½" across. Wrap in waxed paper. Chill until firm.

Heat oven to 400° (mod. hot). Slice ⅛" thick. Bake 8 to 10 min. on ungreased baking sheet.

FRUITCAKE BARS

Ingredients for 3 doz.	Ingredients for 6 doz.
1 cup brown sugar (packed)	2 cups brown sugar (packed)
1¼ cups water	2½ cups water
⅓ cup shortening	⅔ cup shortening
2 cups raisins	4 cups raisins
2 cups Gold Medal Flour	4 cups Gold Medal Flour
1 tsp. salt	2 tsp. salt
1 tsp. soda	2 tsp. soda
1 tsp. baking powder	2 tsp. baking powder
½ tsp. nutmeg	1 tsp. nutmeg
½ tsp. cloves	1 tsp. cloves
2 tsp. cinnamon	1 tbsp. plus 1 tsp. cinnamon
½ cup chopped nuts, if desired	1 cup chopped nuts, if desired
confectioners' sugar	confectioners' sugar
Baking pans	
1 oblong, 13x9½x2"	2 oblongs, 13x9½x2"

Heat oven to 350° (mod.). Mix first four ingredients in saucepan and bring to a boil; remove from heat and cool. Measure flour by dipping method (p. 5) or by sifting. Blend dry ingredients; stir into cooled mixture. Mix in nuts. Spread dough evenly in greased pan(s). Bake 35 to 40 min., or until no imprint remains when touched lightly. Cool; sprinkle with confectioners' sugar. Cut in 2x1½" bars. Store tightly covered to mellow.

PETTICOAT TAILS

Ingredients for 10 doz.

2 cups butter or margarine
2 cups sifted confectioners' sugar
2 tsp. flavoring (vanilla, almond, wintergreen, or rose)
4½ cups Gold Medal Flour
½ tsp. salt

Ingredients for 20 doz.

4 cups butter or margarine
4 cups sifted confectioners' sugar
4 tsp. flavoring (vanilla, almond, wintergreen, or rose)
9 cups Gold Medal Flour
1 tsp. salt

Mix butter, sugar, and flavoring thoroughly. Measure flour by dipping method (p. 5) or by sifting. Mix flour and salt; stir in. Mix with hands. Mold in rolls about 2″ across. Wrap in waxed paper; chill several hours or overnight.

Heat oven to 400° (mod. hot). Cut slices about ⅛″ thick. Place a little apart on ungreased baking sheet. Bake 8 to 10 min., or until lightly browned.

KALEIDOSCOPE COOKIES

We also call these cookies Summer Pastels.

Make dough for Petticoat Tails (above). Divide dough in thirds. Follow directions for 3 variations of your choice (below). Wrap tightly; chill several hours or overnight.

Heat oven to 375° (quick mod.). Hold cookies at room temperature until easy to slice, yet firm. Slice ⅛″ thick. Bake on ungreased baking sheet 7 to 9 min. Do not brown.

Green Cookies

For 3⅓ doz.	For 6⅔ doz.
2 tbsp. finely grated lemon rind	¼ cup finely grated lemon rind
green food coloring	green food coloring
multi-colored sugar	multi-colored sugar

Add lemon rind and food coloring to ⅓ of dough. Roll in multi-colored sugar.

Pink Cookies

For 3⅓ doz.	For 6⅔ doz.
½ to 1 tsp. peppermint extract	1 to 1½ tsp. peppermint extract
red food coloring	red food coloring
red decorators' sugar	red decorators' sugar

Add extract and food coloring to ⅓ of dough. Roll in red decorators' sugar.

Yellow Cookies

For 3⅓ doz.	For 6⅔ doz.
2 tbsp. finely grated orange rind	¼ cup finely grated orange rind
yellow food coloring	yellow food coloring
finely chopped almonds	finely chopped almonds

Add orange rind and food coloring to ⅓ of dough. Roll in finely chopped almonds.

Chocolate Cookies

For 3⅓ doz.	For 6⅔ doz.
2 sq. semi-sweet chocolate (2 oz.), melted	4 sq. semi-sweet chocolate (4 oz.), melted
chocolate shot	chocolate shot

Add melted chocolate to ⅓ of dough. Roll in chocolate shot.

EASY FILLED COOKIES

Ingredients for 5 doz.	Ingredients for 10 doz.
1 cup shortening	2 cups shortening
2 cups brown sugar (packed)	4 cups brown sugar (packed)
2 eggs	4 eggs
½ cup water or buttermilk	1 cup water or buttermilk
1 tsp. vanilla	2 tsp. vanilla
3½ cups Gold Medal Flour	7 cups Gold Medal Flour
1 tsp. salt	2 tsp. salt
1 tsp. soda	2 tsp. soda
⅛ tsp. cinnamon	¼ tsp. cinnamon
Cherry-Pineapple Filling (below)	Cherry-Pineapple Filling (below)

Heat oven to 400° (mod. hot). Mix shortening, sugar, and eggs. Stir in water and vanilla. Measure flour by dipping method (p. 5) or by sifting. Blend remaining ingredients; stir in. Drop dough by teaspoonfuls on greased baking sheet. Place ½ tsp. Filling on dough; cover with ½ tsp. dough. Bake 10 to 12 min.

Cherry-Pineapple Filling

1 can (8½ oz.) crushed pineapple (1 cup including juice)	2 cans (8½ oz. each) crushed pineapple (2 cups including juice)
¼ cup chopped candied or maraschino cherries	½ cup chopped candied or maraschino cherries
½ cup sugar	1 cup sugar
½ cup chopped nuts	1 cup chopped nuts

Mix pineapple, cherries, and sugar; cook until very thick. Add nuts; mix well. Cool.

ORANGE OATMEAL COOKIES

Crispy, crunchy, with pleasing orange tang.

Ingredients for 5 doz.	Ingredients for 10 doz.
2 cups Gold Medal Flour	4 cups Gold Medal Flour
2 cups sugar	4 cups sugar
4 tsp. baking powder	2 tbsp. plus 2 tsp. baking powder
1 tsp. salt	2 tsp. salt
1 tsp. nutmeg	2 tsp. nutmeg
1 cup shortening	2 cups shortening
2 eggs	4 eggs
4 tsp. grated orange rind	2 tbsp. plus 2 tsp. grated orange rind
2 tbsp. orange juice	¼ cup orange juice
3 cups rolled oats	6 cups rolled oats

Heat oven to 375° (quick mod.). Measure flour by dipping method (p. 5) or by sifting. Blend flour, sugar, baking powder, salt, and nutmeg; add shortening, eggs, orange rind, and juice. Mix well. Stir in oats. Drop level tablespoonfuls of dough on greased baking sheet 2″ apart. Bake 12 to 15 min.

PEANUT JUMBLES

Ingredients for 5 doz.	Ingredients for 10 doz.
⅔ cup shortening	1⅓ cups shortening
½ cup peanut butter	1 cup peanut butter
⅔ cup granulated sugar	1⅓ cups granulated sugar
⅔ cup brown sugar (packed)	1⅓ cups brown sugar (packed)
2 eggs	4 eggs
½ cup milk	1 cup milk
1 tsp. vanilla	2 tsp. vanilla
2 cups Gold Medal Flour	4 cups Gold Medal Flour
2 tsp. baking powder	4 tsp. baking powder
1 tsp. salt	2 tsp. salt
1 cup chopped peanuts	2 cups chopped peanuts

Heat oven to 375° (quick mod.). Mix shortening, peanut butter, sugars, and eggs thoroughly. Stir in milk and vanilla. Measure flour by dipping method (p. 5) or by sifting. Blend dry ingredients; stir into shortening mixture. Stir in peanuts. Drop rounded teaspoonfuls of dough 2″ apart on greased baking sheet. Bake 10 to 12 min.

MINCEMEAT BARS

Ingredients for 6 doz.	Ingredients for 12 doz.
1½ cups brown sugar (packed)	3 cups brown sugar (packed)
2 eggs	4 eggs
2 tbsp. molasses	¼ cup molasses
1 tbsp. butter or margarine	2 tbsp. butter or margarine
1 tsp. vanilla	2 tsp. vanilla
2 cups Gold Medal Flour	4 cups Gold Medal Flour
½ tsp. salt	1 tsp. salt
½ tsp. soda	1 tsp. soda
1 tsp. each cinnamon and cloves	2 tsp. each cinnamon and cloves
3 tbsp. hot water	6 tbsp. hot water
¼ cup almonds, slivered	½ cup almonds, slivered
¼ cup raisins	½ cup raisins
1 pkg. (9 oz.) mincemeat, separated	2 pkg. (9 oz. each) mincemeat, separated
1½ cups sifted confectioners' sugar	3 cups sifted confectioners' sugar
about 3 tbsp. hot milk	about 6 tbsp. hot milk
½ tsp. each vanilla and almond flavoring	1 tsp. each vanilla and almond flavoring

Baking pans

2 oblongs, 13x9½x2″	4 oblongs, 13x9½x2″

Heat oven to 400° (mod. hot). Mix brown sugar, eggs, molasses, butter, and vanilla thoroughly. Measure flour by dipping method (p. 5) or by sifting. Blend flour, salt, soda, and spices; stir in. Mix in hot water. Stir in almonds, raisins, and mincemeat. Spread dough thin in greased pans. (Dough puffs and fills in any holes as it bakes.) Bake 12 to 15 min., or until no imprint remains when touched lightly. Spread immediately with mixture of confectioners' sugar, milk, and flavorings. Cut in 2x1½″ bars.

APPLESAUCE RAISIN COOKIES

¾ cup shortening
1 cup brown sugar
   (packed)
1 egg
½ cup applesauce
2¼ cups Gold Medal
   Flour

½ tsp. soda
½ tsp. salt
¾ tsp. cinnamon
¼ tsp. cloves
1 cup raisins
½ cup nuts, chopped

Heat oven to 375° (quick mod.). Mix shortening, sugar, and egg thoroughly. Stir in applesauce. Measure flour by dipping method (p. 5) or by sifting. Blend dry ingredients and stir in. Mix in raisins and nuts. Drop dough by teaspoonfuls on greased baking sheet. Bake 10 to 12 min., or until lightly browned. *Makes 4 doz. cookies.*

Note: *If you use Gold Medal Self-Rising Flour, omit soda and salt.*

BANANA SPICE COOKIES

½ cup shortening
1 cup brown sugar
   (packed)
2 eggs
1 cup mashed bananas
   (about 2)
2 cups Gold Medal
   Flour

2 tsp. baking powder
¼ tsp. soda
¼ tsp. salt
½ tsp. cinnamon
¼ tsp. cloves
½ cup chopped nuts

Mix well shortening, sugar, and eggs. Stir in bananas. Measure flour by dipping method (p. 5) or by sifting. Mix dry ingredients and stir in. Blend in nuts. Chill about 1 hr.

Heat oven to 375° (quick mod.). Drop rounded tablespoonfuls of dough 2″ apart on lightly greased baking sheet. Bake 8 to 10 min. If desired, frost with a thin confectioners' sugar icing. *Makes 3 to 4 doz. cookies.*

Note: *If you use Gold Medal Self-Rising Flour, omit baking powder, soda, and salt.*

APPLESAUCE BROWNIES

Different; applesauce gives a nice cake-like texture.

½ cup shortening
2 sq. unsweetened
   chocolate (2 oz.)
1 cup sugar
2 eggs, well beaten
½ cup applesauce
1 tsp. vanilla

1 cup Gold Medal
   Flour
½ tsp. baking powder
¼ tsp. soda
¼ tsp. salt
½ cup nuts, chopped

Heat oven to 350° (mod.). Melt shortening and chocolate over hot water. Blend in sugar, eggs, applesauce, and vanilla. Measure flour by dipping method (p. 5) or by sifting. Stir dry ingredients together; blend into shortening mixture. Spread batter in greased and floured square pan, 9x9x1¾″. Bake 35 to 40 min., or until top springs back when lightly touched. While hot, cut into 2¼x1½″ bars. *Makes 2 doz. bars.*

Note: *If you use Gold Medal Self-Rising Flour, omit salt, baking powder, and soda.*

CEREAL COCONUT COOKIES

¼ cup shortening
½ cup brown sugar
   (packed)
¼ cup granulated
   sugar
1 egg
¼ tsp. vanilla

1 cup Gold Medal
   Flour
½ tsp. soda
¼ tsp. salt
1 cup coconut
1 cup Jets cereal or
   Wheaties

Heat oven to 375° (quick mod.). Mix thoroughly shortening, sugars, egg, and vanilla. Measure flour by dipping method (p. 5) or by sifting. Blend dry ingredients; stir in. Blend in coconut and cereal. Drop dough by teaspoonfuls on ungreased baking sheet. Bake 8 to 10 min. *Makes 3 doz. cookies.*

Note: *If you use Gold Medal Self-Rising Flour, omit soda and salt.*

WHEATIES DATE BALLS

For "children" of all ages.

½ cup butter or
  margarine
¾ cup sugar
1 lb. pitted dates,
  cut up (2½ cups)
1 egg, well beaten
1 tbsp. milk

½ tsp. salt
1 tsp. vanilla
½ cup chopped nuts
2 cups crushed
  Wheaties (4 cups
  before crushing)
finely chopped nuts or
  coconut

Mix butter, sugar, and dates. Cook over low heat, stirring constantly until butter melts. Remove from heat. Mix egg, milk, salt, and vanilla; add to date mixture. Cook over very low heat, stirring constantly, about 4 min., or until dates are soft and blended in with other ingredients. Remove from heat; stir in nuts. Cool 5 min.; stir in Wheaties. As soon as mixture is cool enough to handle, form into small balls and roll in finely chopped nuts or coconut. *Makes 75 small balls.*

PEANUT-MALLOW CLUSTERS

From Esther Roth of our staff, who says that they are a favorite with her husband's investment club.

1 pkg. (6 oz.) semi-
  sweet chocolate
  pieces
1 sq. unsweetened
  chocolate (1 oz.)
1 tbsp. butter or
  margarine
2 eggs

1¼ cups confectioners'
  sugar
½ tsp. salt
1 tsp. vanilla
2 cups salted peanuts
2 cups miniature
  marshmallows

Melt chocolate pieces, chocolate square, and butter in top of double boiler over hot water. Beat eggs until foamy; stir in sugar, salt, and vanilla. Blend egg mixture with chocolate mixture. Stir in peanuts and marshmallows. Drop by rounded teaspoonfuls on waxed paper. Refrigerate 1 hr. to set. *Makes 4 doz. clusters.*

ROCKY ROAD CHOCOLATE BARS

For cool cooking, try this bar that is a cross between a brownie and fudge.

1 pkg. (6 oz.) semi-
  sweet chocolate
  pieces (1 cup)
¾ cup evaporated milk
1 cup chopped nuts
2 cups miniature
  marshmallows

4 cups graham cracker
  crumbs (52 sq.) or
  crushed Kix cereal
1 cup confectioners'
  sugar

Add chocolate to milk in small saucepan. Cook, stirring constantly, over low heat until chocolate is melted and sauce is smooth. Mix nuts, marshmallows, crumbs, and sugar in large bowl. Pour chocolate over crumb mixture; mix until all crumbs are moistened. Turn into well-buttered square pan, 9x9x1¾"; press down in even layer. Chill until firm. Sprinkle with confectioners' sugar, if desired. Cut in bars. *Makes 2 doz. bars.*

CREAM PRALINES

1 lb. light brown sugar (2¼ cups)
⅛ tsp. salt
¾ cup evaporated milk

2 tbsp. butter or margarine
2 cups pecan halves (½ lb.)

Mix sugar, salt, milk, and butter in 2-qt. saucepan. Cook, stirring constantly, over low heat until sugar is dissolved. Add pecans and cook over medium heat to soft ball stage (234° on candy thermometer), stirring constantly. Remove from heat; let cool 5 min. Stir rapidly until mixture begins to thicken and coats pecans. Working quickly, drop by teaspoonfuls on lightly buttered baking sheet, forming patties. If candy stiffens and is slightly rough looking before all patties are formed, soften and restore gloss by adding a few drops of hot water. Let stand until cool and set. *Makes about 4 doz. pralines.*

BUTTER CRUNCH CONFECTION-COOKIES

Also delicious for dessert; slice ½" thick and top with whipped cream. See color picture, pp. 56-57.

1 pkg. (8 oz.) dates, chopped
½ cup water

Butter Crunch (below)
1 can (4 oz.) coconut, toasted

Cook dates in water until thick. Cool. Fold in 2¼ cups Butter Crunch and toasted coconut. Roll into cylinder (2" wide); roll in rest of Butter Crunch to coat outside. Refrigerate several hours or overnight. Slice about ¼" thick for cookies. *Makes 2 to 3 doz. cookies.*

Butter Crunch

½ cup butter or margarine
¼ cup brown sugar (packed)

1 cup Gold Medal Flour
½ cup chopped pecans or walnuts

Heat oven to 400° (mod. hot). Measure flour by dipping method (p. 5) or by sifting. Mix all ingredients with hands. Spread in ungreased oblong pan, 13x9½x2". Bake 15 min. Take from oven; stir with spoon. Cool. *Makes 2½ cups.*

PEANUT BUTTER DATE BALLS

1 cup peanut butter
1 cup confectioners' sugar
1 cup chopped nuts (walnuts or peanuts)

1 cup chopped dates
1 tbsp. butter or margarine
¾ bar (4-oz. bar) German sweet chocolate

Mix peanut butter, sugar, nuts, dates, and butter well. Break chocolate into top of double boiler and let it melt while shaping dough into marble-sized balls. With metal spatula or knife, spread top of balls with melted chocolate and swirl, giving bonbon effect. Refrigerate until set. *Makes about 110 balls.*

Note: *If chunk-style peanut butter is used, use only ¾ cup chopped nuts.*

PEANUT BUTTER DATE MINIATURES

Follow recipe for Peanut Butter Date Balls (above) —except pat dough into ungreased square pan, 9x9x1¾"; spread with 1 bar (4 oz.) German sweet chocolate, melted. Refrigerate until set; cut into 1" squares. *Makes about 81 squares.*

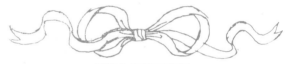

KIX TOFFEE

Crisp, buttery toffee, mixed with Kix. Brittle, but at the same time melt-in-your-mouth.

1 cup butter or margarine

1 cup sugar
2½ cups Kix cereal

Mix butter and sugar in heavy skillet or shallow saucepan. Cook over medium heat, stirring constantly, until mixture caramelizes (becomes light brown in color and has a heavy consistency), 20 to 25 min. Be sure to keep stirring constantly. Remove from heat. Stir in Kix. Turn out mixture on baking sheet; spread to ¼" thickness. Let cool; break into pieces.

CHOCOLATE KIX TOFFEE

Make Kix Toffee (above)—except immediately after spreading toffee out on baking sheet, place six 1-oz. milk chocolate bars over the hot candy. As it melts, spread the chocolate over the toffee.

HOLIDAY APRICOT BALLS

1 pkg. (8 oz.) dried apricots, ground or finely cut	¾ cup sweetened condensed milk
2½ cups flaked coconut	1 cup finely chopped nuts

Blend apricots, coconut, and milk well. Shape in small balls. Roll in chopped nuts. Let stand about 2 hr. to firm. *Makes about 5 doz. balls.*

Note: *Apricot Balls may be stored uncovered at room temperature for 3 or 4 days.*

TANGY APRICOT BALLS

Make Holiday Apricot Balls (above) adding 2 tbsp. lemon juice to the coconut mixture.

APRICOT-NUT BALLS

Make Holiday Apricot Balls (above)—except add the nuts to the mixture; roll balls in confectioners' sugar.

UNBAKED DATE WALNUT SQUARES

2 cups cut-up pitted dates (¾ lb.)	¼ cup butter or margarine, melted
¾ cup water	2 tbsp. sugar
2 tbsp. sugar	1 tsp. vanilla
2 tbsp. lemon juice	½ tsp. cinnamon
¾ cup chopped walnuts	¼ tsp. salt
1½ cups graham cracker crumbs (20-2½″ sq.)	¼ cup chopped walnuts

Blend dates, water, 2 tbsp. sugar, and lemon juice in saucepan. Cook over low heat, stirring constantly, until soft and thick, about 5 min. Remove from heat; stir in ¾ cup walnuts; cool. Blend crumbs, butter, 2 tbsp. sugar, vanilla, cinnamon, and salt. Press ¾ crumb mixture on bottom of greased square pan, 8x8x2″. Spoon cooled filling evenly over entire surface. Add ¼ cup walnuts to remaining ¼ crumb mixture; sprinkle evenly over filling. Press entire surface firmly with fingers. Chill about 3 hr., or until firm enough to cut. *Makes about 5 doz. 1″ squares.*

ROSETTES

Perfect rosettes are crisp yet tender.

½ cup Gold Medal	½ cup water or milk
Flour	1 egg, slightly beaten
1 tbsp. sugar	1 tbsp. vegetable oil
½ tsp. salt	confectioners' sugar

Measure flour by dipping method (p. 5) or by sifting. Blend dry ingredients together. Mix remaining ingredients; stir in. Strain mixture. Heat rosette iron in hot fat (400°) 3″ deep in small saucepan. Tap off excess fat on absorbent paper. Dip into batter until ⅔ covered. Immerse in hot fat. Fry until delicately browned. Remove; tip upside-down to drain. Push off rosette.

Heat iron in fat again; repeat process. If iron is too cool, batter will slip off into fat; if iron is too hot, batter will stick. Stir batter each time before dipping in iron. Sprinkle rosettes with confectioners' sugar. (Best if made only a day or two before served.) Store rosettes in single layers in waxed paper-lined boxes. *Makes 18 rosettes.*

Note: *If you use Gold Medal Self-Rising Flour, omit salt.*

BUTTERY NUT ROUNDS

Heat oven to 350° (mod.). Make dough for Russian Teacakes (p. 54). Roll dough about ¼″ thick (rather less than more) on lightly floured cloth-covered board. Cut with cooky cutter 1½″ in diameter. Place on ungreased baking sheet. Bake 10 to 12 min., or until set but not browned. Cool. Sprinkle with confectioners' sugar, frost with a bitter chocolate icing, or stack together with raspberry jam. *Makes 8 doz. cookies.*

LEBKUCHEN

Traditional Christmas honey cakes from the Black Forest region of Germany.

½ cup honey	½ tsp. soda
½ cup molasses	1 tsp. cinnamon
¾ cup brown sugar	1 tsp. cloves
(packed)	1 tsp. allspice
1 egg	1 tsp. nutmeg
1 tbsp. lemon juice	⅓ cup cut-up citron
1 tsp. grated lemon	⅓ cup chopped nuts
rind	Glazing Icing (below)
2¾ cups Gold Medal	
Flour	

Mix honey and molasses; bring to a boil. Cool thoroughly. Stir in sugar, egg, lemon juice, and rind. Measure flour by dipping method (p. 5) or by sifting. Stir dry ingredients together; blend in. Mix in citron and nuts. Chill dough overnight.

Heat oven to 400° (mod. hot). Roll small amount of dough at a time, keeping rest chilled. Roll out ¼″ thick on lightly floured board; cut in oblongs, 2½x 1½″. Place 1″ apart on greased baking sheet. Bake 10 to 12 min., or until no imprint remains when touched lightly. Brush Icing lightly over cookies immediately. Quickly remove from baking sheet. Cool and store in airtight container with cut orange or apple for a few days to mellow. *Makes 6 doz. cookies.*

Note: *Do not use Gold Medal Self-Rising Flour in this recipe.*

Glazing Icing: Blend 1 cup sugar and ½ cup water in small saucepan. Boil until first indication of thread appears (230° on candy thermometer). Remove from heat. Stir in ¼ cup confectioners' sugar. If icing becomes sugary while brushing cookies, reheat slightly, adding a little water until clear again. Any leftover icing may be used on fruitcake or other fruit bars.

COCONUT-CHOCOLATE MERINGUE BITES

From Diana Williams of San Francisco, formerly of our staff. See color picture, p. 17.

¾ cup butter
 or margarine
½ cup brown sugar
 (packed)
½ cup granulated
 sugar
3 eggs, separated
1 tsp. vanilla
2 cups Gold Medal
 Flour
1 tsp. baking powder

¼ tsp. soda
¼ tsp. salt
1 pkg. (6 oz.) semi-
 sweet chocolate
 pieces
1 cup flaked or grated
 coconut
¾ cup coarsely
 chopped nuts
1 cup brown sugar
 (packed)

Heat oven to 350° (mod.). Grease an oblong pan, 13x9½x2″. Mix butter, ½ cup brown sugar, granulated sugar, egg yolks, and vanilla. Beat 2 min. medium speed on mixer or 300 vigorous strokes by hand, scraping bowl constantly. Measure flour by dipping method (p. 5) or by sifting. Blend flour, baking powder, soda, and salt together; mix in thoroughly. Spread or pat dough in pan. Sprinkle with chocolate pieces, coconut, and nuts. Beat egg whites until frothy; add 1 cup brown sugar gradually; beat until stiff. Spread over nuts. Bake 35 to 40 min. Cool; cut in bars. *Makes 40 to 60 bars.*

Note: *If you use Gold Medal Self-Rising Flour, omit baking powder, soda, and salt.*

CHOCOLATE ORANGE DROPS

½ cup shortening (part
 butter or
 margarine)
1 pkg. (3 oz.) cream
 cheese
½ cup sugar
1 egg
1 tsp. grated orange
 rind

1 tsp. vanilla
1 cup Gold Medal
 Flour
½ tsp. salt
1 pkg. (6 oz.) semi-
 sweet chocolate
 pieces

Heat oven to 350° (mod.). Mix shortening, cream cheese, sugar, egg, orange rind, and vanilla thoroughly. Measure flour by dipping method (p. 5) or by sifting. Blend flour and salt together; stir into shortening mixture. Stir in chocolate pieces, mixing thoroughly. Drop dough by teaspoonfuls about 1″ apart on lightly greased baking sheet. Bake about 15 min. Edges will be delicately browned. *Makes about 3 doz. cookies.*

Note: *If you use Gold Medal Self-Rising Flour, omit salt.*

FANCY FILBERT BARS

Specialty of Jeannette Campbell Ludcke from Minneapolis, wife of a busy executive and mother of three.

½ cup shortening (half
 butter or
 margarine)
½ cup sifted
 confectioners'
 sugar
2 egg yolks

1 cup Gold Medal
 Flour
½ to ¾ cup currant
 or raspberry jelly
Meringue-Filbert
 Topping (below)

Heat oven to 350° (mod.). Mix shortening, sugar, and egg yolks thoroughly. Measure flour by dipping method (p. 5) or by sifting. Stir in flour. Press and flatten with hand to cover bottom of ungreased oblong pan, 13x9½x2″. Bake 10 min. Spread with softened jelly, then with Topping. Bake 20 min. more, or until Topping is golden brown. Cool slightly; cut in bars. *Makes about 2½ doz. 3x1″ bars.*

Note: *You may use Gold Medal Self-Rising Flour in this recipe.*

Meringue-Filbert Topping: Beat 2 egg whites until frothy. Gradually add ½ cup sugar and ¼ tsp. cinnamon; beat until stiff and glossy. Fold in 1 cup finely chopped filberts (unblanched).

VANILLA REFRIGERATOR COOKIES

1 cup shortening	1½ tsp. vanilla
½ cup granulated sugar	2¾ cups Gold Medal
½ cup brown sugar	Flour
(packed)	½ tsp. soda
2 eggs	1 tsp. salt

Mix shortening, sugars, eggs, and vanilla thoroughly. Measure flour by dipping method (p. 5) or by sifting. Blend dry ingredients together; mix into shortening mixture. Mix thoroughly with hands. Press and mold into a long, smooth roll about 2½" in diameter. Wrap in waxed paper; chill several hours or overnight.

Heat oven to 400° (mod. hot). Cut in thin slices (⅛ to 1/16" thick). Place a little apart on ungreased baking sheet. Bake 6 to 8 min., or until lightly browned. *Makes about 6 doz. 2½" cookies.*

Note: *If you use Gold Medal Self-Rising Flour, omit salt; reduce soda to ¼ tsp.*

NUT REFRIGERATOR COOKIES

Make Vanilla Refrigerator Cookies (above)—except mix ½ cup cut-up nuts into dough.

CINNAMON SLICES

Make Vanilla Refrigerator Cookies (above)—except use 2 to 3 tsp. cinnamon in place of vanilla.

DATE-NUT REFRIGERATOR COOKIES

Make Vanilla Refrigerator Cookies (above)—except mix ½ cup finely cut dates and ½ cup finely chopped nuts into dough.

CHOCOLATE SLICES

Make Vanilla Refrigerator Cookies (above)—except blend 2 sq. unsweetened chocolate (2 oz.), melted and cooled, into shortening mixture.

OATMEAL COCONUT CRISPIES

1 cup shortening (part	2½ cups Gold Medal
butter or margarine)	Flour
1 cup granulated sugar	1 tsp. soda
1 cup brown sugar	1 tsp. salt
(packed)	1 cup rolled oats
2 eggs	1 cup flaked coconut
1 tsp. vanilla	

Mix shortening, sugars, eggs, and vanilla until fluffy. Measure flour by dipping method (p. 5) or by sifting. Blend flour, soda, and salt thoroughly; stir into shortening mixture. Blend in rolled oats and coconut. (Dough will be soft.) Shape in 2 rolls, each about 2" in diameter. Wrap in waxed paper; refrigerate overnight.

Heat oven to 400° (mod. hot). Cut in ¼" slices. Place on lightly greased baking sheet. Bake 10 to 12 min., or until lightly browned. *Makes about 7 doz. cookies.*

Note: *If you use Gold Medal Self-Rising Flour, omit soda and salt.*

OATMEAL COCONUT DROPS

Make Oatmeal Coconut Crispies (above)—except use only 1¾ cups Gold Medal Flour; drop dough by rounded teaspoonfuls on lightly greased baking sheet.

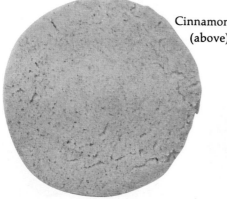

Cinnamon Slices
(above)

Oatmeal Coconut
Crispies (above)

Easy Chinese Almond Cookies
(p. 33)

DATE-OATMEAL COOKIES

Try these golden crispy rounds for a pleasant change from the old standby, oatmeal-raisin cookies.

¾ cup shortening (half butter or margarine)	2 cups Gold Medal Flour
1 cup brown sugar (packed)	¾ tsp. soda
2 eggs	1 tsp. salt
3 tbsp. milk	2 cups rolled oats
1 tsp. vanilla	1½ cups cut-up dates
	¾ cup chopped nuts

Mix shortening, sugar, eggs, milk, and vanilla thoroughly. Measure flour by dipping method (p. 5) or by sifting. Blend flour, soda, and salt; stir in. Mix in oats, dates, and nuts. Chill.

Heat oven to 375° (quick mod.). Roll dough in 1¼" balls. Place 3" apart on lightly greased baking sheet. Flatten to ¼" thickness with bottom of glass dipped in flour. Bake 10 to 12 min., or until lightly browned. *Makes 4 doz. 2½" cookies.*

Note: *If you use Gold Medal Self-Rising Flour, omit soda and salt.*

RUSSIAN TEACAKES

Sometimes called Mexican Wedding Cakes. See color picture, pp. 56-57.

1 cup butter or margarine	2¼ cups Gold Medal Flour
½ cup sifted confectioners' sugar	¼ tsp. salt
1 tsp. vanilla	¾ cup finely chopped nuts

Mix butter, sugar, and vanilla thoroughly. Measure flour by dipping method (p. 5) or by sifting. Stir flour and salt together; blend in. Mix in nuts. Chill dough.

Heat oven to 400° (mod. hot). Roll dough in 1" balls. Place on ungreased baking sheet. (Cookies do not spread.) Bake 10 to 12 min., or until set but not brown. While still warm, roll in confectioners' sugar. Cool. Roll in sugar again. *Makes about 4 doz. 1" cookies.*

Note: *Do not use Gold Medal Self-Rising Flour in this recipe.*

BRIEF MOMENTS

Make dough for Russian Teacakes (above) omitting nuts. Form ½ teaspoonfuls of dough into kiss shape. Bake in 400° oven 8 to 10 min. When cool, put two together (flat sides) with tinted Easy Creamy Icing (p. 60). *Makes 7 doz. cookies.*

COCKLE SHELLS

Make dough for Russian Teacakes (above) omitting nuts. Divide dough in half. Color half coral (¼ tsp. red food coloring and 7 drops yellow food coloring); leave remaining half white. Chill dough. Put together 1 level tsp. coral dough and 1 level tsp. white dough. Roll into pencil-like roll. (If dough becomes soft or sticky, roll on lightly floured surface.) Shape roll in a coil on baking sheet. Bake about 8 min. *Makes 40 cockle shells.*

Cooky-Candies (p. 55)

Cockle Shells (above)

Russian Teacakes (above)

CREAM FILBERT CANDY COOKIES

A Christmas cooky that resembles creamed filberts (mothball candies).

1 cup shortening (part butter or margarine)	1/8 tsp. salt
	1 tsp. vanilla
	2 to 3 oz. filberts
3/4 cup sugar	Glaze (below)
1 egg	60 sugar cubes, crushed,
2 1/2 cups Gold Medal Flour	or coarse granulated sugar
1/2 tsp. baking powder	

Heat oven to 375° (quick mod.). Cream shortening and sugar. Add egg. Measure flour by dipping method (p. 5) or by sifting. Stir dry ingredients together. Blend into creamed mixture. Add vanilla. Roll in balls (using 1 level tsp. dough per ball) and press a filbert in center. Shape so dough covers nut. Place on ungreased baking sheet about 2″ apart. Bake 12 to 15 min., until delicately browned. Cool. Holding cooky at bottom, dip entire top in Glaze. Roll cooky in crushed sugar. *Makes 7 to 8 doz. cookies.*

Note: *If you use Gold Medal Self-Rising Flour, omit baking powder and salt.*

Glaze: Mix 2 cups sifted confectioners' sugar, 3 tbsp. water, and 2 tsp. vanilla.

COOKY-CANDIES

Rich oatmeal shortbread-type cooky with festive toppings. Also called Sprinkle-Top Cookies.

1 cup butter or margarine	1/2 cup rolled oats
	1/2 cup semi-sweet chocolate pieces
3/4 cup sifted confectioners' sugar	1/4 cup milk
1 tbsp. vanilla	finely chopped pecans or walnuts
2 cups Gold Medal Flour	shredded coconut
3/4 tsp. salt	chocolate shot

Heat oven to 325° (slow mod.). Mix butter, sugar, and vanilla well. Measure flour by dipping method (p. 5) or by sifting. Stir flour, salt, and rolled oats into butter mixture.

With fingers, shape teaspoonfuls of dough into rounds, balls, crescents, triangles, and bars. Bake on ungreased baking sheet 20 to 25 min., or until golden around edges. (Watch baking time. These are easily overbaked.) Cool.

Melt chocolate; add milk; blend until smooth. Dip cookies, rounded-side-down, in chocolate; then dip in nuts, coconut, or chocolate shot. *Makes about 4 doz. cookies.*

Note: *Do not use Gold Medal Self-Rising Flour in this recipe.*

CHRISTMAS COOKY
GIFT CONTAINERS

Coffee Cans: Cover cans with gay Christmas gift wrap, gluing it to the can and lid with all-purpose glue. For a 1-lb. can, you will need a circle 5″ in diameter for lid top, a piece of matching gift tie 16¼″ long to glue around edge of lid, and a strip of paper 3¼″ wide and 16¼″ long to glue around can. For a 2-lb. can, sizes for lid are the same, strip to go around can should be 6½″ high.

Another attractive way to decorate coffee cans is spray painting. Easy-to-use aerosol cans of paint are available in a wide variety of colors—and the paint dries in seconds. You could spray the can red or green, then letter "Merry Christmas" with gold ink and a small paint brush. For a gift can that could be used to store cookies the year round, choose a color that will harmonize with your friend's kitchen, adding a holiday touch with ribbons and a pine cone.

Rolled Oats or Corn Meal Boxes: Adhesive-backed paper is handy for covering boxes like these. After covering, decorate with rickrack, lace edging, or designs cut from last year's Christmas cards—all glued in place.

Beautiful four-color holiday photographs cut from women's magazines make unusual coverings, too.

Plastic Freezer Boxes: Plastic containers for refrigerator or freezer use make perfect gift containers for cookies. You can bake cookies and fill boxes, then store in freezer; only the gift wrapping is left for the busy pre-holiday days.

Apothecary Jars: For your prettiest, most colorful cookies, use apothecary jars (inexpensive copies of the famous old containers used in apothecary shops). You may want to trim the jar with gold braid or tiny shells glued in designs. Or pack the cooky-filled jar in a box and gift-wrap the box.

Russian Teacakes (p. 54)

Holiday Fruit Drops

Chocolate Crinkles (p. 58)

Butter Crunch Confection-Cookies (p. 49)

Kaleidoscope Cookies (p. 44)

How to Make Perfect Molded Cookies

Mix dough as directed. Richer, softer doughs call for chilling before shaping. Roll into balls between palms of hands. Bake as balls or flatten with bottom of glass or by crisscrossing with fork.

For attractive crescents, fruits, candy canes, etc., take your time and mold cookies carefully. As you become more skillful, molding will go more quickly.

Perfect molded cookies have:
- *uniform shape*
- *delicate brown exterior*
- *crisp, tender eating quality*
- *pleasing flavor*

SNICKERDOODLES

The recipe for this delicious "family cooky" came to us from Mrs. Ronald Anfinson, Benson, Minnesota.

1 cup shortening (part butter or margarine)	2 tsp. cream of tartar
1½ cups sugar	1 tsp. soda
2 eggs	¼ tsp. salt
2¾ cups Gold Medal Flour	2 tbsp. sugar
	2 tsp. cinnamon

Heat oven to 400° (mod. hot). Mix shortening, 1½ cups sugar, and eggs thoroughly. Measure flour by dipping method (p. 5) or by sifting. Blend flour, cream of tartar, soda, and salt; stir in. Shape dough in 1″ balls. Roll in mixture of 2 tbsp. sugar and cinnamon. Place 2″ apart on ungreased baking sheet. Bake 8 to 10 min. These cookies puff up at first, then flatten out. *Makes 6 doz. cookies.*

Note: *If you use Gold Medal Self-Rising Flour, omit cream of tartar, soda, and salt.*

CHOCOLATE CRINKLES

See color picture, pp. 56-57.

½ cup vegetable oil	2 tsp. vanilla
4 sq. unsweetened chocolate (4 oz.), melted	2 cups Gold Medal Flour
	2 tsp. baking powder
	½ tsp. salt
2 cups granulated sugar	1 cup confectioners' sugar
4 eggs	

Mix oil, chocolate, and granulated sugar. Blend in one egg at a time until well mixed. Add vanilla. Measure flour by dipping method (p. 5) or by sifting. Stir flour, baking powder, and salt into oil mixture. Chill several hours or overnight.

Heat oven to 350° (mod.). Drop teaspoonfuls of dough into confectioners' sugar. Roll in sugar; shape into balls. Place about 2″ apart on greased baking sheet. Bake 10 to 12 min. Do not overbake! *Makes about 6 doz. cookies.*

Note: *If you use Gold Medal Self-Rising Flour, omit baking powder and salt.*

Snickerdoodles (above)

Chocolate Crinkles (above)

TOFFEE SQUARES

Rich cooky that looks and tastes like toffee candy. Especially good at holiday time.

1 cup butter or margarine	2 cups Gold Medal Flour
1 cup brown sugar (packed)	¼ tsp. salt
1 egg yolk	3 to 4 milk chocolate bars (⅞ oz. each)
1 tsp. vanilla	½ cup chopped nuts

Heat oven to 350° (mod.). Mix butter, sugar, egg yolk, and vanilla. Measure flour by dipping method (p. 5) or by sifting. Stir in flour and salt until dough is well blended. Spread in a rectangle about 13x10″ on greased baking sheet, leaving about 1″ all around edge of baking sheet. Bake 20 to 25 min., or until nicely browned. (For a softer cake-like cooky, spread dough in an oblong pan, 13x9½x2″; bake 25 to 30 min.) Crust will still be soft. Remove from oven. Immediately place separated squares of chocolate on top. Let stand until soft; spread evenly over entire surface. Sprinkle with nuts. Cut in small squares while warm. *Makes 6 to 7 doz. squares.*

Note: *If you use Gold Medal Self-Rising Flour, omit salt.*

BUTTERSCOTCH TOFFEE SQUARES

Make Toffee Squares (above)—except while crust bakes, melt and blend 1 pkg. (6 oz.) butterscotch pieces, ¼ cup light corn syrup, 2 tbsp. shortening, 1 tbsp. water, and ¼ tsp. salt over hot water. Spread this (instead of softened chocolate) over entire surface.

SNOWFLAKES

½ cup sugar	1¼ cups Gold Medal Flour
⅓ cup butter or margarine	½ tsp. baking powder
1 egg	½ tsp. salt
½ tsp. vanilla	sweet chocolate, melted pistachio nuts, chopped

Mix sugar, butter, egg, and flavoring well. Measure flour by dipping method (p. 5) or by sifting. Stir dry ingredients together and blend into shortening mixture. Chill 1 hr.

Heat oven to 400° (mod. hot). Roll dough ⅛″ thick on floured board. Cut into small stars. Bake on ungreased baking sheet 6 to 8 min., until lightly browned. Cool. Put two cookies together with melted sweet chocolate; add dab of chocolate and sprinkling of chopped pistachio nuts on top. *Makes 32 cookies.*

Note: *If you use Gold Medal Self-Rising Flour, omit baking powder and salt.*

CHRISTMAS STOCKINGS

1 cup shortening (part butter or margarine)	2¼ cups Gold Medal Flour
½ cup sifted confectioners' sugar	½ tsp. salt
1 tsp. vanilla	9 candied cherries, quartered
½ tsp. almond flavoring	¼ cup broken nuts
¼ to ½ tsp. red or green food coloring	¼ cup semi-sweet chocolate pieces
	Easy Creamy Icing (p. 60)

Mix shortening, sugar, flavorings, and food coloring well. Measure flour by dipping method (p. 5) or by sifting. Blend flour and salt; stir into shortening mixture. Chill 1 hr.

Heat oven to 400° (mod. hot). In palm of hand, pat 1 level tbsp. dough into oblong about 3x1½″. If dough seems to be too dry, carefully add a few drops of cream. Lengthwise down center, place "surprises"— 2 chocolate pieces, 1 cherry quarter, 2 pieces of nuts. Mold dough around "surprises" and shape into roll 3″ long. Place on ungreased baking sheet, turning end of roll to form foot of stocking. Bake 10 to 12 min. Cool. Ice tops and toes. *Makes about 3 doz. stockings.*

Note: *Do not use Gold Medal Self-Rising Flour in this recipe.*

EASY CREAMY ICING

1 cup sifted	½ tsp. vanilla or other
confectioners' sugar	flavoring
¼ tsp. salt	1½ tbsp. cream or
	1 tbsp. water

Blend sugar, salt, and flavoring (try lemon, almond, or peppermint flavoring for variety). Add cream to make easy to spread. If desired, tint with a few drops of food coloring. Spread on cookies with spatula or pastry brush. *Makes icing for 3 to 5 doz. cookies, depending on size.*

HINT

For professional looking iced drop cookies, place 1 tsp. icing on center of each cooky. With small icing spatula, spread icing with circular motion.

MARIE'S CHOCOLATE ICING

1 tbsp. butter	1½ tbsp. warm water
1 sq. unsweetened	1 cup sifted
chocolate (1 oz.)	confectioners' sugar

Melt butter and chocolate over hot water. Blend in warm water. Beat in confectioners' sugar until icing spreads easily. *Makes icing to frost 9" sq. pan of cookies or 3 to 4 doz. cookies.*

BUTTER ICING

2½ tbsp. soft butter	1½ tbsp. cream
1½ cups sifted	¾ tsp. vanilla
confectioners' sugar	

Blend butter and sugar together. Stir in cream and vanilla until smooth. *Makes icing for 4 doz. cookies.*

BROWNED BUTTER ICING

Make Butter Icing (above)—except brown butter in saucepan over medium heat until a delicate brown. Blend with sugar.

ORANGE BUTTER ICING

Make Butter Icing (above)—except use 1½ tbsp. orange juice and 2 tsp. grated orange rind in place of cream and vanilla.

LEMON BUTTER ICING

Make Butter Icing (above)—except use 1½ tbsp. lemon juice and 2 tsp. grated lemon rind in place of cream and vanilla.

MOCHA BUTTER ICING

Make Butter Icing (above)—except omit cream and vanilla and blend in 1 tsp. powdered instant coffee dissolved in 1 tbsp. hot water. If icing is too thick to spread, add a few drops

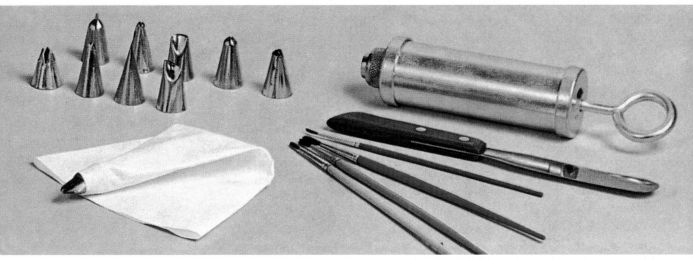

QUICK CREAM ICING

Blend 1½ cups sifted confectioners' sugar, ¼ tsp. vanilla, and enough cream (2 to 3 tbsp.) to make a thin icing. *Makes icing for 15x10" pan of cookies.*

DECORATOR ICING

Combine 1½ to 2 cups sifted confectioners' sugar with a small amount of egg white or water (1 to 2 tbsp.— just enough to make icing easy to force through decorating tube yet hold its shape).

BROWNED BUTTER GLAZE

¼ cup butter   **½ tsp. vanilla**
1 cup sifted   **1 to 2 tbsp. hot water**
  confectioners' sugar

Melt butter until golden brown. Blend in sugar and vanilla. Stir in hot water until icing spreads smoothly. *Makes icing for about 30 cookies.*

THIN CONFECTIONERS' SUGAR ICING

Mix 1 cup sifted confectioners' sugar; 1 to 2 tbsp. milk, water, or cream; and ½ tsp. vanilla until smooth.

PEANUT BUTTER ICING

Delicious on Chocolate Slices (p. 53).

2 tbsp. chunk-style   **1½ cups sifted**
  peanut butter   **confectioners'**
2 to 3 tbsp. milk   **sugar**

Stir all ingredients together until creamy.

FROSTING "CEMENT"

For our charming Cooky House (pp. 14-15).

2 egg whites   **2 cups sifted**
½ tsp. cream of tartar   **confectioners' sugar**
    food coloring

Using electric mixer, beat egg whites with cream of tartar until stiff. Gradually beat in 1 cup of sugar. Beat 10 min. Beat in second cup of sugar; beat 10 min. more. During last few minutes of beating, add food coloring for desired color. While using or storing the frosting "cement," press transparent plastic wrap directly on top of frosting in bowl to prevent drying; lift wrap just long enough to remove "cement" for each application.

THIN CHOCOLATE ICING

1 sq. unsweetened   **1 cup sifted**
  chocolate (1 oz.)   **confectioners' sugar**
1 tsp. butter   **2 tbsp. boiling water**

Melt chocolate and butter together over hot water. Remove from heat. Blend in sugar and water. Beat only until smooth but not stiff.

OUT OF CHOCOLATE?

If you run out of chocolate, use cocoa. Substitute 3 tbsp. cocoa plus 1 tbsp. butter or margarine for 1 sq. unsweetened chocolate.